simple crochet

simple crochet

ERIKA KNIGHT

photographs by

John Heseltine

Quadrille
PUBLISHING

dedication

In celebration of everyone who goes
beyond function and practicality, for
the passion of their craft.

Created and produced by Susan Berry and Erika Knight
for Quadrille Publishing Ltd
Publishing Director Jane O'Shea
Editor Sally Harding
Designer Anne Wilson
Photographer John Heseltine
Stylist Julia Bird
Production Director Vincent Smith

First published in 2003 by
Quadrille Publishing Limited
Alhambra House
27–31 Charing Cross Road
London WC2H 0LS
www.quadrille.co.uk

Reprinted in 2004 (twice), 2006, 2008, 2010, 2013
10 9 8 7

Quadrille
craft

www.quadrillecraft.co.uk

British Library Cataloguing-in-Publication Data
A catalogue record for this book is available from
the British Library.

ISBN 978 184400 015 9

Printed in China

contents

introduction

As we begin to reassess our lifestyles, we will find inspiration at home and in traditional values. Cherishing the personal and the hand-made is part of this, as we seek to surround ourselves with things that are precious to us. Hand-made textiles offer a unique opportunity to express our creativity in simple yet enduring ways, and there is no easier form of this than crochet. Basic yet intricate, delicate yet robust, practical yet decorative, it creates a fabric that has a beautiful and interesting texture. Moreover, as I hope this book demonstrates, it is also amazingly versatile.

'I believe in making things simple and in making simple things.'

Crochet is much easier than knitting, using only one hook and a ball of yarn, and it is easy to carry around, so you can do it anywhere – on the train, the bus, the plane, in your lunch break or while waiting for your children in the playground. With only a little practice you will find your fingers working to a rhythm. You can crochet while you chat to friends or listen to the radio or to music, so you make the best use of your increasingly precious time. It is, undoubtedly, a form of yoga for the hands.

Simple Crochet is what it says. It concentrates on a few basic stitches, and some very different types of yarn. With just this, you are able to make almost anything. Moreover, crochet is quick; most of the projects in this book take only a few evenings at most. So, with luck, you will actually finish a project! Too many of us have embarked on crafts we have found complicated, and the half-finished remnants still lurk in the back of our cupboards and wardrobes.

'You can create a fabric with crochet from almost any length of continuous fibre.'

String, rags and leather – you name it, you can crochet with it. The materials are easy to locate, you can even find them in the garden shed or the hardware store as well as in the local yarn shop. Experimenting is the key. Feel the different textures, the natural touch, and have fun with non-traditional materials, too. The fabric that crochet makes is firm and textural, but endlessly versatile. The projects I have chosen for this book, I hope, make crochet modern and interesting. Use crochet imaginatively to create textiles that offer a visual surprise: mix delicate items with modern, hard-edged surfaces or combine tough string cushions with delicate antique linen, for example.

But most important of all, in making crochet, you create something that is very much your own – personal, beautiful and long lasting.

Release your creativity!

Erika Knight

yarns

1

2

5

6

9

8

10

You can crochet with a wonderful range of yarns, to produce some excitingly varied textiles. The yarn and stitch chosen will determine the character of the crochet. Examples are shown on pages 10-11.

below Just some of the yarns at your disposal, including soft cotton (**1**), hemp (**2**), metallic thread (**3**), heavy-weight string (**4**), ribbon (**5**), leather (**6**), linen (**7**), thick cotton (**8**), dyed cotton (**9**), natural cotton (**10**), fine cotton (**11**) and mohair (**12**).

3

4

7

8

11

12

9

texture

Crochet is one of the most basic forms of textile, having at its roots an affinity with fisherman's nets and medieval lace. The inspiration for this book is the very different materials with which you can crochet using only the most basic, easy-to-work stitches. Crochet can be worked in rows or in the round, and squares or strips of crochet can be joined together to make patchworks or throws.

You can use the texture of crochet in many ways, sometimes with dramatic results. Some projects in this book have been made from unusual materials: leather, raffia or string. Some have a tight, dense and firm structure, while others are more open and flexible. For the latter, yarns such as metallic thread or mercerized cotton are ideal. Woven effects can be created for functional rugs and throws – using old fabrics cut into strips works brilliantly for this kind of texture. To emphasize the versatility of crochet, you can even create sculptural items using tough yarns such as sisal or hemp.

The choice of yarn and fabric will be determined by the form and function of the textile. A floor cushion requires a heavy-duty, robust thread that will stand plenty of wear and tear. Leather is a great choice as its appearance improves with wear, but it is not the cheapest of materials. Sisal and hemp are less expensive and look good, too, as do strips of fabric cut from old denim jeans and jackets, for example, both tough enough for hard-wearing longevity.

The samples, right, show you the variations in texture and form that can be achieved using a variety of different threads and yarns.

Soft cotton is light and warm. It is ideal for soft, flexible fabrics for cushions or throws.

Leather has a brilliant sheen and is very durable. Use it for stylish interiors, in the form of containers or floor cushions.

Ribbon makes a soft, elegant, feminine-looking fabric that is cool and lightweight. Use it for cushions or throws.

Thick cotton is soft, smooth and very warm. It has great stitch clarity. Use it for blankets and throws.

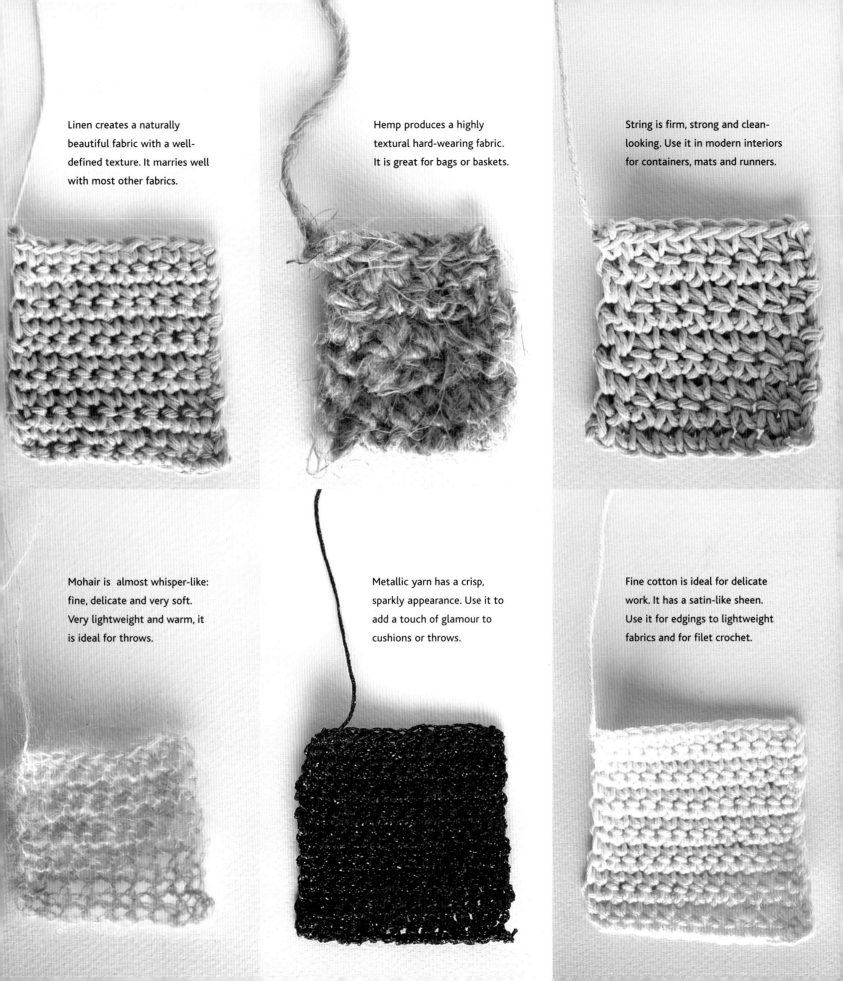

Linen creates a naturally beautiful fabric with a well-defined texture. It marries well with most other fabrics.

Hemp produces a highly textural hard-wearing fabric. It is great for bags or baskets.

String is firm, strong and clean-looking. Use it in modern interiors for containers, mats and runners.

Mohair is almost whisper-like: fine, delicate and very soft. Very lightweight and warm, it is ideal for throws.

Metallic yarn has a crisp, sparkly appearance. Use it to add a touch of glamour to cushions or throws.

Fine cotton is ideal for delicate work. It has a satin-like sheen. Use it for edgings to lightweight fabrics and for filet crochet.

colour

Choosing appropriate colours is both exciting and challenging. My own colour palette tends towards natural colours and monochromes as a base, with touches of brighter colour to give it life and lustre. I find that this works well in most interior schemes, and provides a bridge between contemporary style and the much-loved pieces of furniture that all of us gather as our lives progress.

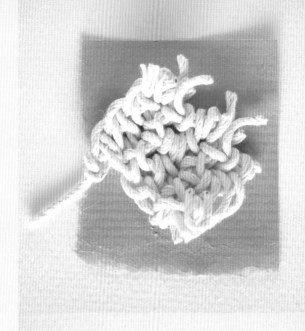

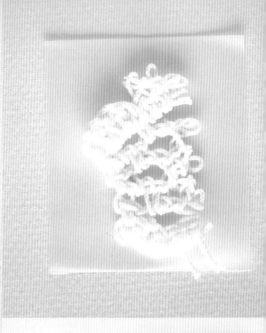

NATURAL COLOURS

In the natural colour palette, undyed yarns, simple parcel string, and cool monochromes work well with modern interiors – light woods, glass, leather, brick, plaster and metal. If you have a minimalist interior, this palette will complement it, but the textiles will add a necessary touch of softness and luxury. Texture adds sparkle to a surface, particularly when you use contrasts: matt with shiny, thick with thin, and soft with hard. Combine metallic yarns with leather, for example, or use soft linen on bleached wood or glass.

COLOUR WITH NATURAL

In the colour with natural palette, you can add small touches of colour to neutrals to provide 'hot spots' in an otherwise simple scheme. Add a bright border to a plain throw or container, add stripes of strong reds or pinks to a runner with a neutral ground, or add toning borders or stripes in soft greens and browns.

COLOUR ON COLOUR

To create vibrancy, my personal passion is for pinks and greens in every hue, which work with the natural palette and also give a traditional look a modern twist, especially when spiced with a dash of orange or mango, or with just a hint of pomegranate. Clash colours, and keep the surprises coming!

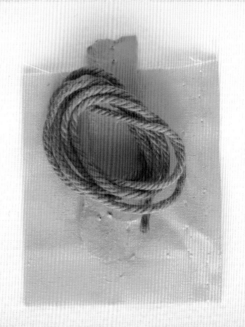

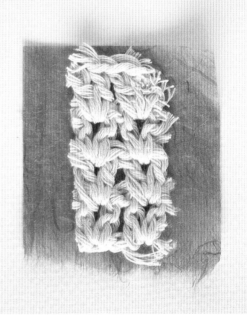

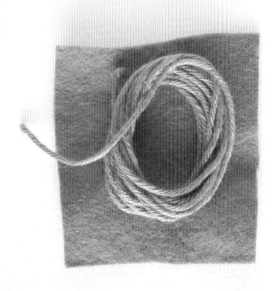
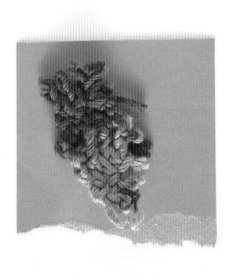

crochet basics

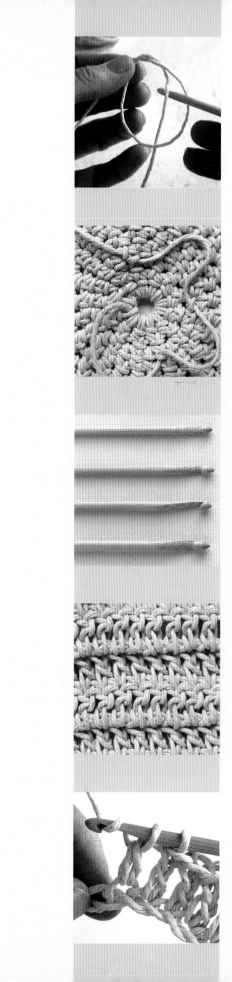

equipment & tension

You really need very little equipment for crochet. The most important item is the crochet hook. I like to work with bamboo hooks, because not only are they made from a natural material, they have a very smooth finish, so that the yarn slides easily over the tip.

It is important when crocheting to feel very comfortable with the way you hold the hook and yarn, and you should practise the basic techniques shown on pages 18-27 until you are comfortable with the process.

The hooks come in various sizes, from very fine (.60mm) to very thick (16.00mm). Those shown opposite are the most commonly used sizes in this book. Fine threads will usually require a fine hook, while chunky cottons or string need the larger sizes.

In addition to your hooks, you will need a large-eyed sewing needle with a blunt tip (a 'yarn' or 'tapestry' needle) and a pair of sharp dressmakers' scissors. A tape measure or ruler is useful too.

tension

Everyone who makes textiles works with a different tension. Your 'tension' is how tightly or loosely you make the crochet loops (your stitch size). This means that the size of the stitch will vary from crocheter to crocheter, even when the same yarn and hook size is used. Crochet patterns are designed with a specific stitch size in mind, so it is best to test your stitch size before starting your crochet project – otherwise it may turn out bigger or smaller than planned.

In the patterns that follow (as in most crochet patterns) the stitch size is measured over 10cm/4in horizontally and vertically, counting both rows and stitches.

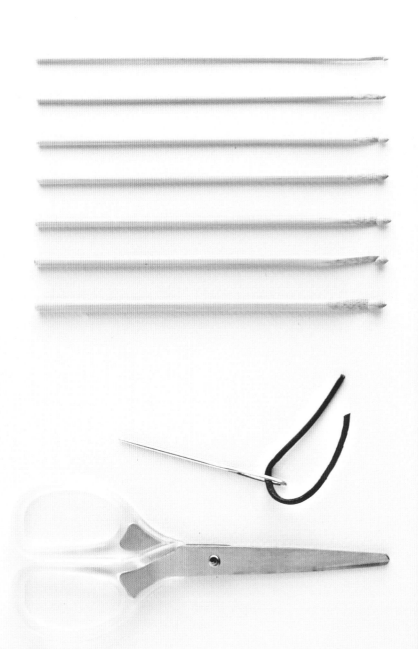

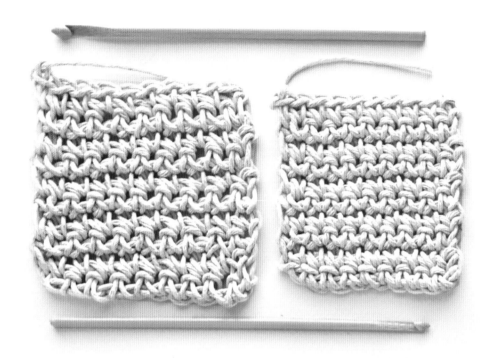

left The basic equipment required is a crochet hook, a blunt-ended sewing needle and sharp scissors. The hooks shown left (top to bottom) show the grades from 2.00mm to 5.00mm.

right To test your stitch size (or tension), make a piece about 13cm (5in) square in the required stitch, using the recommended yarn and hook size (bottom right). Count the number of rows and the number of stitches over the given measurement (usually 10cm/4in). If these accurately match those of the tension specified in your pattern, you can safely use the recommended hook size. But if you find that you get too many stitches, change to a size larger hook and try again. If you get too few stitches, change to a size smaller hook and try again. The difference one hook size larger or smaller will make to the stitch size in the sample, right, is shown top left and top right respectively.

starting to crochet

To crochet easily and successfully, you need to hold the yarn and the hook comfortably, with enough tension on the yarn so that when you draw the hook around the yarn, it stays firmly in the lip of the hook. To this end, most people choose to wrap the yarn around their fingers, and some make an additional wrap around their little finger – choose whatever yarn-holding method that works best for you. Similarly, hold the hook in whatever way you find most comfortable. Some favour a pencil grip, while others hold the hook between their thumb and forefinger like a knife. You may even prefer to change your grip depending on the type of stitch you are working at the time or on the size of the hook.

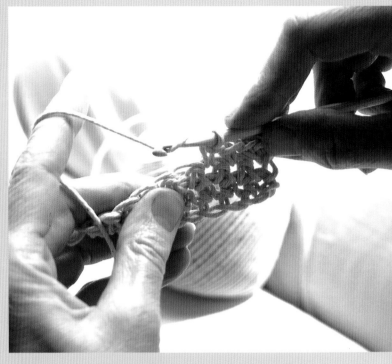

holding yarn/hook
method one

Wrap the ball end of the yarn around the little finger of your left hand, over the third finger, behind the second and over the forefinger. When you are starting to crochet, leave a long, loose tail end of yarn on the palm side of your hand. Hold the hook in your right hand like a pencil.

holding yarn/hook
method two

Wrap the ball end of the yarn between the little finger of your left hand, behind the third and second fingers, and over the forefinger. When you are starting to crochet, leave a long, loose tail end of yarn on the palm side of your hand. Hold the hook in your right hand like you would a knife.

making the first loop

To start to crochet, you first need to make a slip loop. There are many different ways in which you can do this, but the method shown below is very easy to follow. You can, of course, devise your own system if you prefer.

step one

one   Make a loop in the tail end of the yarn as shown, crossing the tail end of the yarn over the ball end.

two   Let the tail end drop down behind the loop, then pass the crochet hook over the loop on the right, catch it with the hook and pull it through loop.

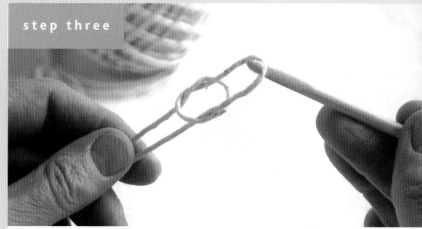

step three

three   Holding the tail end and the ball end of the yarn in your left hand, start to pull the hook in the opposite direction to create a loop on the hook.

four   Keep pulling the yarn until the first loop forms on the hook, with a tight knot under it.

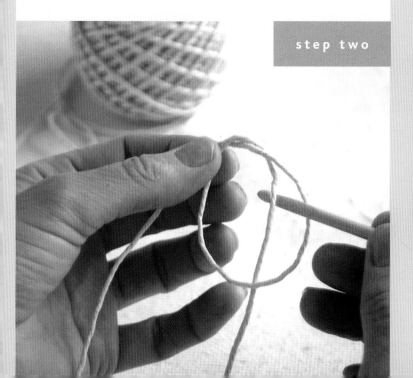

step two

step four

making a foundation chain

After you have made the slip loop on your hook, the next step is to create the foundation for the crochet fabric. This is called the 'foundation chain'. Your crochet instructions will tell you how many chain to make to start. Chain stitches are also used at the beginning of a row and for lace patterns.

step one

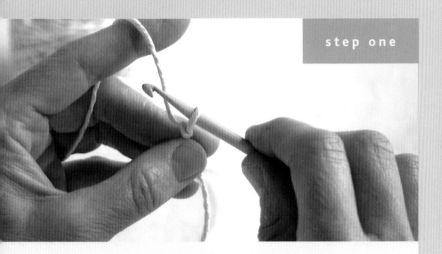

one   With the slip loop on the hook and the yarn held taut in your left hand, grip the tail end of the yarn. To begin the chain stitch, pass the tip of the hook in front of the yarn, then under and around it.

two   Keeping the yarn taut, catch the yarn in the lip of the hook, then draw it through the loop on the hook as indicated by the arrow.

step two

three   This completes the first chain and leaves you with a loop still on the hook. To make your next chain pull a new loop through the loop on the hook. Keep the chain stitches slightly loose as you will be working into them on your first row.

step three

four   Make the number of chain required. You should be able to count them easily, as each one makes a neat entity, with a visible smooth front, and more twisted back.

step four

Slip stitch is also known as 'single crochet'. If you work it into the foundation chain and continue making row after row of it, it forms a very dense, unyielding fabric. It is more commonly used to join the end and beginning of a round, or to work invisibly along the top of other stitches until you reach the required position.

three This completes the first slip stitch and leaves one loop on the hook. Work the next slip stitch into the next chain in the same way. If you intend to work into the slip stitches on the next row, then work them fairly loosely.

step three

step one

one Make a foundation chain (see previous page). Holding the end of the chain between the thumb and second finger of the left hand and tensioning the yarn over the forefinger of the left hand, insert the tip of the hook through the second chain from the hook as shown by the arrow.

two Catch the yarn with the hook (called 'wrap the yarn around the hook') and draw it through the chain and the loop on the hook.

four Continue working a slip stitch into each chain to the end. To begin a second slip stitch row, turn the work at the end of the first row. Then make one chain and work a slip stitch into the top of each stitch of the previous row.

step four

step two

double crochet

Double crochet is sometimes also known as 'plain stitch'. It creates a dense but still flexible fabric, which is ideal for hardwearing, strong textiles. The easiest of all crochet fabrics to make, it is used frequently in this book in an exciting range of yarn textures, including soft cotton yarn, rags, string and leather. Double crochet and chain stitches can be combined to form other, softer fabrics.

step one

one Make your foundation chain. Then insert the hook through the second chain from the hook (see step 1 of slip stitch on previous page). Wrap the yarn around the hook and pull a loop through the chain as shown.

two There are now two loops on the hook. Wrap the yarn around the hook and pull a loop through both of these loops.

three This completes the first stitch. To make the next stitch, insert the hook through the next chain, draw a loop through, then draw a loop through both loops on the hook.

four Work a double crochet into each of the remaining chain in the same way to complete your first row.

second row

To start your second row of double crochet, turn the work so the loop on the hook is at the right edge. You will then have to make a 'turning' chain to take the yarn up to the correct height.

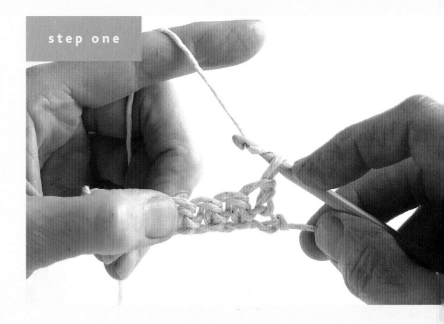

one At the beginning the second row, draw a loop through the loop on the hook to form a loose chain.

two Inserting the hook through both loops at the top of the stitch, work a double crochet into each double crochet of the previous row. Work following rows in the same way as the second row.

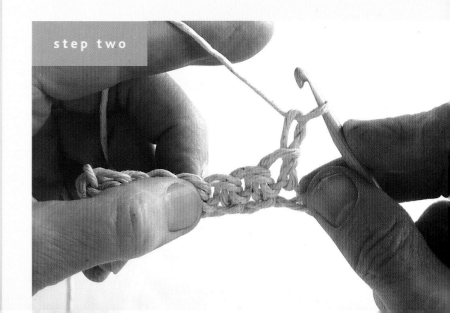

treble crochet

Treble crochet is taller than double crochet. It results in a stitch that is more open and less dense, so it is a flexible, soft textile. It is worked in much the same way as double crochet, except that you wrap the yarn around the hook before beginning the stitch. And as it is taller, you begin the first row by working into the fourth chain from the hook.

step one

o n e Make the number of foundation chain your require. Then wrap the yarn around the hook as shown and insert the hook into the fourth chain from the hook.

t w o There are now three loops on the hook. Wrap the yarn around the hook and draw a loop through the first two loops on the hook (first arrow), leaving two loops on the hook. Next, wrap the yarn around the hook and draw it through the remaining two loops on the hook (second arrow).

t h r e e This completes the first treble. Wrap the yarn around the hook to begin the second treble and work it into the next chain in the same way.

f o u r Work a treble into each chain to the end. Then turn the work to begin the next row. Make three chain at the beginning of the second row – this is called the 'turning' chain and counts as the first stitch of the row. Miss the first stitch in the row below and work the first treble into the top of the next stitch. At the end of the row work the last stitch into the top of the three-chain at the edge. Work following rows as for the second.

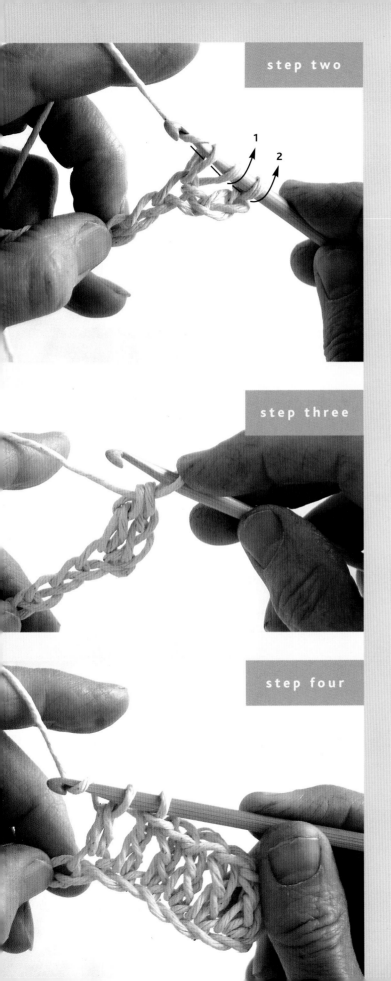

step two

step three

step four

half treble & double treble

The two remaining basic crochet stitches are half treble and double treble. A half treble is slightly shorter than a treble, and a double treble slightly taller. Try them out following the instructions below, and you'll know all you need to know to work simple crochet pattern stitches!

half treble

half treble Work in exactly the same way as treble, except in step 1 insert the hook into the third chain from the hook and in step 2 draw a single loop through all three loops on the hook to complete the stitch. In the second row work two turning chain instead of three.

double treble Work in exactly the same way as treble, except in step 1 wrap the yarn twice around the hook and insert the hook into the fifth chain from the hook, and in step 2 draw a loop through two loops on the hook three times instead of twice. In the second row work four turning chain instead of three.

double treble

working in rounds

Some circular pieces require you to work in rounds rather than rows. The stitches may vary but the basic technique is the same. To begin, you will need to make a ring of a few chain as the foundation. Yarn thickness will determine how many chain you make, but generally for a hole at the centre that is drawn closed, about four to six chain will do.

step three

step one

o n e   Make six chain, then insert the hook through the first chain made. Wrap the yarn around the hook in the usual way, then draw a loop through the chain and the loop on the hook as for a slip stitch. This forms a ring of chain.

t w o   If you are working double crochet into the ring, start by making one chain. (Make three chain if your first round is trebles, two for half treble or four for double treble.)

t h r e e   Inserting you hook into the ring (not into the chain), work as many stitches into the ring as your instructions tell you. Catch the loose end of yarn into the stitches of the first round so you can use it to pull the hole tight later. When you work in rounds the right side is always facing you, so don't 'turn' the work at the end of the round.

f o u r   Before starting the second round of stitches, mark the beginning of the round – when working in rounds, it is sometimes hard to tell where one round ends and the next begins, so it is a good idea to position a marker here. Place a short length of a contrasting yarn across your crochet from front to back. Put it tight up against the loop on the hook as shown. When the second round is started the marker will be caught in postiton under the top of the first stitch and show you clearly where the round was begun. Pull out and reposition the marker at the end of each following round.

step two

step four

new yarns

If you want to start a new ball of yarn when the old one runs out, or when changing to a new colour for stripes or for any other colour pattern, there is no need to fasten off first. You can just keep crocheting and draw the new yarn in when it is needed. There's nothing to it!

step one

o n e   When working in double crochet, begin the stitch in the usual way by inserting the hook into the next stitch and drawing a loop through. Then drop the old yarn, pick up the new yarn and wrap it around the hook. Draw a loop of the new yarn through the two loops on the hook to complete the double crochet. With other stitches, join in a new yarn in the same way – with the last loop of the stitch.

t w o   Work over the ends of the new and old yarn for several stitches, then neatly clip off the ends close to the fabric.

step two

finishing

Once you have completed a piece of work, you will need to fasten it to stop it from unravelling. This is also known as 'casting off'. To neaten your finished crochet pieces, weave all the loose ends of yarn into the fabric.

fastening off

fastening off

To fasten off, cut off the yarn leaving about l5cm/6in or so. Then draw the loose end through the loop on the hook and pull tight.

weaving in

To weave in ends, thread the yarn into a blunt-ended needle with a suitably large eye, run the needle through several stitches near it, and then snip off the excess yarn.

weaving in

cushions

round cushion

The back and front of this simple, contemporary string cushion are worked round and round in a continuous, spiralling row of double crochet. To keep the cushion flat you gradually build up the number of stitches in each round. It produces a firm, dense fabric.

CUSHION SIZE
Approximately 40cm/16in in diameter.

MATERIALS
4 x 89m/98yd balls thick parcel string (from hardware stores or stationers)
Hook size 4.00mm
Round cushion pad 40cm/16in in diameter (or customize a square pad – see Tips)
Length of contrasting coloured yarn for marker

STITCH SIZE
This cushion has a 'tension' (stitch size) of 15 stitches and 20 rows to 10cm/4in measured over double crochet worked in parcel string, but working to an exact tension is not essential (see Tips).

TECHNIQUES USED
Double crochet, working in rounds and joining in new balls of yarn.

TIPS
Working in rounds
When you work your crochet in rounds you never have to turn the fabric. The right side is always facing you.

Tension
Don't worry about tension too much! Because this string cushion cover is made in circles, you can just keep working your stitches in a spiral until it is the required size.

Marking the beginning of a round
Be sure to mark the beginning of each round to make it easier to keep your place.

Joining in a new yarn
This technique is used for changing yarns when your ball of yarn is finished or when you want to start a new colour for stripes. Begin a double crochet in the usual way, by drawing a loop through the next stitch, then drop the old yarn and draw the new yarn through both loops now on the hook to finish the double crochet (see Crochet Basics). Leave long loose ends of the old and new yarns to weave in later, or work over the ends of the old yarn for several stitches before clipping them off.

Making a round cushion pad
Customize a square cushion pad to fit, by first chalking a 40cm/16in circle on the pad. Then take each corner in turn, shake the stuffing to the middle of the pad, fold down the empty corners, and stitch through both layers along the chalked line.

METHOD
Foundation-chain ring Leaving a long loose end and using a 4.00mm hook, make 6 chain and join length of chain into a ring by working a slip stitch into first chain made.

Round 1 (right side) Make 1 chain, work 12dc into ring, working over long loose end.

If you wish, you can make this simple cushion in a random colour mix. The one shown right was worked in cotton in three colours: cream, beige and green. To create a similar cushion, simply follow the pattern, and work in the new yarns randomly to create this informal effect, following the instructions on page 27 for joining in new yarn. If you wish to create a cushion with regular circular stripes, add the new colours at the start of each appropriate round. You could vary the thickness of the stripes, and the colours, to suit your own design.

Before starting the next round, place a short length of a contrasting yarn across your crochet fabric from front to back, tight up against the loop on the hook and above the working yarn. Then start to work the double crochet of *round 2*, catching the marker in position. The marker will show you where the round started, as it will be caught under the top of the first stitch of the round.

Round 2 (right side) 1dc into each of 12dc of previous round, making sure you are no longer working over loose end. At the end of each round pull the marker out and place it across your crochet fabric, up against the loop on the hook as before, so it will always be under the top of the first stitch of the round showing you where to start the next round.

Round 3 Work 2dc into each dc to end. There are now 24dc in the circle.

Round 4 Work 1dc into each dc to end.

Round 5 1dc into first dc, 2dc into next dc, *1dc into next dc, 2dc into next dc, repeat from * to end. 36dc.

Rounds 6 and 7 As round 4.

Round 8 1dc into each of first 2dc, 2dc into next dc, *1dc into each of next 2dc, 2dc into next dc, repeat from * to end. 48dc.

Rounds 9 and 10 As round 4.

Round 11 1dc into each of first 3dc, 2dc into next dc, *1dc into each of next 3dc, 2dc into next dc, repeat from * to end. 60dc.

Rounds 12 and 13 As round 4.

Round 14 1dc into each of first 4dc, 2dc into next dc, *1dc into each of next 4dc, 2dc into next dc, repeat from * to end. 72dc. Continue in this way, working two rounds without increases followed by one round with 12 evenly spaced increases, until circle measures 40cm/16in across (about 40 rounds).

Slip stitch into next stitch and fasten off. Work another circle the same.

TO FINISH

Pull the long loose end at the centre of each circle to tighten up the hole and weave it in on the wrong side of the work. Weave in any other loose ends on the wrong side as well.

Lay the circles out flat, then steam and press lightly.

Sew the circles together or join with double crochet as follows:

Join the circles with dc

Place the circles together with the wrong sides facing each other, line up the stitches along the outside edge and pin. Work 1dc through a dc at the edge of the two layers. Continue like this, working 1dc through each dc and making sure you catch in both layers with each stitch. When the opening is just large enough to insert the cushion pad, push it inside and finish the edging. Fasten off and weave in the end.

chevron cushion

This cushion is a reinvention of a popular '60s pattern. You can try out different colourways or group the stripes in varying pattern widths. The cushion is worked in bands of contrasting colours with a splash of metallic thread, but it looks good, too, when worked in a single colour. Combine several plain or patterned versions to add a touch of glamour to a plain sofa or armchair.

making : the chevron cushion

CUSHION SIZE
Approximately 40cm/15³/4in square.

MATERIALS
Rowan *Cotton Glacé* or a similar medium-weight mercerized cotton yarn (see page 122) in 4 contrasting colours as follows:
Colour A: 2 x 50g balls in terracotta
Colour B: 2 x 50g balls in off-white
Colour C: 2 x 50g balls in rose pink
Colour D: 1 x 50g ball in burgundy
Twilleys *Goldfingering* or a similar fine metallic yarn (see page 122) in one colour as follows:
Colour E: 1 x 25g ball in claret red
Hook size 3.00mm
Cushion pad 40cm/15³/4in square

STITCH SIZE
This cushion has a 'tension' (stitch size) of 2 chevrons to 11.5cm/4¹/2in and 9 rows to 10cm/4in measured over chevron

pattern, but working to an exact tension is not essential (see Tips).

TECHNIQUES USED
Treble crochet, double crochet, working 3 treble together and joining in new balls of yarn.

TIPS
Tension
Don't worry about tension too much! If your cushion cover ends up a bit bigger or smaller, just buy a cushion pad to fit.
Joining in a new yarn
This technique is used for changing yarns when your ball of yarn is finished or when you want to start a new colour or texture. Change to the new yarn at the end of a row on the cushion. Begin the last treble in the usual way, but change to the new yarn when drawing through the last loop of the stitch. Leave a long loose end of the old

and new yarns to weave in later, or work over the ends for several stitches before clipping them off.

INSPIRATION
Experiment with different yarn textures or different colour combinations, or try various widths of chevron stripes. For a cushion worked entirely in one colour, just follow the instructions for the striped version, but work all 36 rows in the same colour.

METHOD
Foundation chain Leaving a long loose end and using a 3.00mm hook and colour A (terracotta), make 74 chain.
Row 1 Work 1tr into 4th ch from hook, *1tr into each of next 3ch, [yarn round hook and insert hook into next ch, yarn round hook and draw a loop through, yarn round hook and draw through first 2 loops

on hook] 3 times, yarn round hook and draw through all 4 loops on hook—this completes *3tr together*—, 1tr into each of next 3ch, 3tr into next ch, repeat from * to the end, but finishing with only 2tr into last ch instead of 3tr. Turn.

Row 2 Work 3ch, 1tr into first tr, *1tr into each of next 3tr, [yarn round hook and insert hook into next tr, yarn round hook and draw a loop through, yarn round hook and draw through first 2 loops on hook] 3 times, yarn round hook and draw through all 4 loops on hook—this completes *3tr together*—, 1tr into each of next 3tr, 3tr into next tr, repeat from * to end, but finishing last repeat with 2tr (instead of 3tr) into top of turning chain (instead of into a tr). Turn.

Repeating *row 2*, work 2 rows more in colour A.

Stripe pattern
Continuing to repeat *row 2* for chevron pattern, work 32 rows more in stripe pattern as follows:

Colour B (off-white): 1 row.
Colour E (metallic used double): 1 row.
Colour B (off-white): 1 row.
Colour C (rose pink): 2 rows.
Colour D (burgundy): 2 rows.
Colour A (terracotta): 2 rows.
Colour D (burgundy): 2 rows.
Colour B (off-white): 4 rows.
Colour C (rose pink): 1 row.
Colour B (off-white): 1 row.
Colour C (rose pink): 4 rows.
Colour E (metallic used double): 1 row.
Colour A (terracotta): 4 rows.
Colour B (off-white): 1 row.
Colour D (burgundy): 1 row.

Colour B (off-white): 1 row.
Colour C (rose pink): 2 rows.
Colour A (terracotta): 1 row.
Fasten off.
Make another piece the same.

TO FINISH
Weave in any loose ends on the wrong side of the work.
Lay the pieces out flat, then steam and press lightly.

Join the squares with dc
Place the two pieces together with the wrong sides facing each other, line up the stitches along the outside edge and pin. Work a double-crochet edging through both layers to join them. For an even edging, work 1dc between the stitches along the foundation-chain edge and along the last row; 2dc into each row end (around the treble or turning chain) along the sides; and 3dc into each corner to keep the pieces square. Make sure you catch in both layers with each stitch and when the opening is just large enough to insert the cushion pad, push it inside and finish the edging.
Fasten off and weave in the end.

floor cushion

The ultimate in new crochet, this elegant floor cushion is worked in leather. However, the design is so simple and effective that any material could be used instead. Follow the basic pattern principal – four large squares of double crochet joined together to form a giant square. The textural elegance of the design is enhanced by double-crochet seams that are worked on the right side of the fabric to provide a smart finishing touch. The crochet top is stitched to a toning velvet cushion casing.

making : the floor cushion

CUSHION SIZE

The crochet top is approximately 68cm/ 27in square. (The cushion is approximately 68cm/27in square by 9.5cm/3³/4in deep.)

MATERIALS

9 x 50m/55yd balls 2mm-thick round leather thonging or alternative yarn
Hook sizes 9.00mm and 8.00mm
1.5m/1³/4yd cotton velvet 112cm/44in wide and matching sewing machine thread
Zipper (optional)
Cushion pad to fit (see size above)
Strong sewing thread

STITCH SIZE

This cushion has a 'tension' (stitch size) of 8 stitches and 10 rows to 10cm/4in measured over double crochet, but working to an exact tension is not essential (see Tips).
Each square of double crochet measures about 33cm/13¹/4in square.

TECHNIQUES USED

Double crochet and joining in new balls of yarn.

TIPS

Tension

Don't worry about tension too much! Because this is a cushion, making it to an exact size is not important. Just make sure the four patches are square and complete the crocheted top first, then make the fabric cushion cover to fit it.

Joining in a new yarn

This technique is used for starting a new ball of yarn when the one you are using runs out. Begin a double crochet in the usual way, by drawing a loop through the next stitch, then drop the old yarn and draw the new yarn through both loops now on the hook to finish the double crochet (see Crochet Basics). Leave a long loose end of the old and new yarns to weave in later, or work over the ends for several stitches before clipping them off.

Leather

Leather thonging is available at craft stores or from leather merchants. It is quite hard on the hands, so concentrate on one stitch at a time, as a unique aspect of constructing a special textile. Warm the leather in your hands as you work to

soften it. It can be a little sticky, too, and a little talcum powder on the hook may assist to pull it through.

Ready-made cushion

There are instructions for making your own velvet cushion, but if you like, buy a ready-made cushion and make your crochet top to fit it.

INSPIRATION

Use string or chunky felted yarn for less expensive yet equally effective alternatives. Work a little tension square (see Crochet Basics) to find out how many stitches and rows you need.

METHOD

Square (make 4)

Foundation chain Leaving a long loose end and using a 9.00mm hook and leather thonging, make 26 chain.
Change to an 8.00mm hook and begin working in double crochet as follows:
Row 1 Work 1dc into 2nd chain from hook, 1dc into each of remaining chain. Turn.
Row 2 1ch (this counts as first dc of row, so work it loosely), miss first dc and work

1dc into next dc, then work 1dc into each
of remaining dc, work last dc into 1-ch at
edge. Turn. There are 26 stitches in the row.
Repeat *row 2* until work measures
33cm/13$^{1}/_{4}$in from foundation-chain edge
– a total of about 33 rows from beginning.
Fasten off.

TO FINISH

Weave any loose ends into work.
Arrange the four crocheted pieces on a flat
surface so that they form a large square,
with the direction of the rows changing on
every alternate square.
Using an 8.00mm hook and leather, join
the squares together with double crochet
on the right side of the fabric.

Edging

With the right side facing and using an
8.00mm hook and leather, work a row of
dc all around the outside of the finished
square. For an even edging, work 1dc into
each foundation chain or stitch top; 1dc
into each row end; and 3dc into each
corner to keep the piece square. Fasten off.

FABRIC COVER

From the cotton velvet fabric, cut two
pieces 71cm/28$^{1}/_{4}$in square and four
pieces 12.5cm/5in by 71cm/28$^{1}/_{4}$in.
With the right sides together and stitching
1.5cm/$^{5}/_{8}$in from the edge, stitch the
pieces together to make a 'box' – the two
large squares form the top and bottom
and the smaller oblongs the four sides –
leaving one of the long side seams open.
Turn the cover right side out. If desired,
insert a zipper in the opening. Otherwise,
insert the cushion pad and join the seam.
Attach the crocheted leather square to the
top of the cover with strong thread.

textured cushion

This cushion represents a sophisticated twist on a traditional pattern. Metallic yarns are used to create a simple contemporary textile for modern interiors. The cushion front is worked in a lacy stitch that is much easier to crochet than it looks, and the back is worked in plain double crochet. Work several cushions in different types of yarn to create a beautiful textural statement that works equally well on an ultra-modern couch or an antique leather armchair. You could create contrasts with completely different textures, such as suede, velvet or string, if you prefer.

CUSHION SIZE

Approximately 43cm/17¼in square.

MATERIALS

11 x 25g balls Twilleys *Goldfingering* or a similar fine metallic yarn (see page 122)
Hook sizes 3.00mm and 3.50mm
Covered cushion 45cm/18in square

STITCH SIZE

The cushion front has a 'tension' (stitch size) of 5½ V-stitches and 10 rows to 10cm/4in measured over V-stitch pattern. The cushion back has a 'tension' (stitch size) of 22 stitches and 30 rows measured over double crochet (see Tips).

TECHNIQUES USED

Treble crochet, working into a chain space, double crochet and joining in new balls of yarn.

TIPS

Tension

Don't worry about tension too much! If your cushion front ends up a bit bigger or smaller than the size given here, just adjust the size of the double-crochet back pieces to suit it and buy a cushion to fit.

Joining in a new yarn

This technique is used for joining in a new ball of yarn when the one you are using runs out. Begin your treble in the usual way, but change to the new ball of yarn when drawing through the last loop of the stitch. Leave a long loose end of the old yarn and the new yarn to weave in later.

Tightening the back opening

Be sure to change to a size smaller hook before working the last 2.5cm/1in of each back piece. This 'snaps up' the edges and keeps them firm and even.

Buying a covered cushion

For a subtle effect, buy a covered cushion that closely matches the colour of your chosen yarn. If you are good at sewing, you can buy a cushion pad and cover it with a fabric of your choice.

INSPIRATION

Experiment with various colours and yarn textures, such as silk, ribbon or linen. Different yarns will give different stitch sizes, so just adjust the number of foundation chain to get the size you want. The cluster pattern needs a multiple of 9 foundation chain plus 3 extra.

METHOD

Front

Foundation chain Leaving a long loose end and using a 3.50mm hook, make 111 chain.

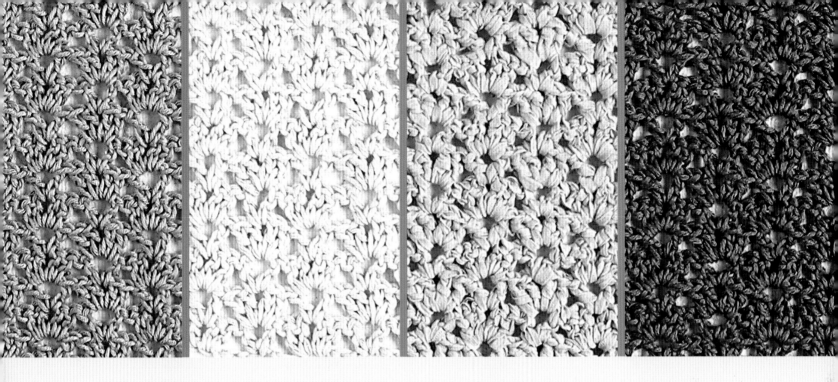

Row 1 Work 2tr into 5th chain from hook, 1ch, 2tr into next ch, miss 3ch, [1tr, 2ch, 1tr] all into next ch, *miss 3ch, 2tr into next ch, 1ch, 2tr into next ch, miss 3ch, [1tr, 2ch, 1tr] all into next ch, repeat from * to last 2ch, miss 1ch, 1tr into last ch. Turn.

Row 2 Work 3ch to count as first tr, [2tr, 1ch, 2tr] into first 2-ch space (inserting hook *under* the chain – not *into* the chain – when working the trebles), [1tr, 2ch, 1tr] into next 1-ch space, *[2tr, 1ch, 2tr] into next 2-ch space, [1tr, 2ch, 1tr] into next 1-ch space, repeat from * to last 2tr, miss these 2tr, 1tr into next ch (top of turning chain). Turn. There are 24 V-stitches across the row (twelve 2tr V-stitches and twelve 4tr V-stitches).

Repeat *row 2* until cushion front measures 43cm/17¼in from foundation-chain edge (a total of about 43 rows from beginning). Fasten off.

Back (worked in 2 pieces)
Foundation chain Leaving a long loose end and using a 3.50mm hook, make 96 chain.

Row 1 Work 1dc into 2nd chain from hook, 1dc into each of remaining chain. Turn. There are 95dc in the row.

Row 2 1ch, 1dc into each dc to end. Turn.

Repeat *row 2* until the work measures 24cm/9½in from foundation-chain edge. Change to 3.00mm hook and work 2.5cm/1in more in dc.
Fasten off.
Make a second piece the same.

TO FINISH
Weave any loose ends into the work.
Lay the pieces out flat, then steam and press lightly.
Place back pieces on a flat surface and overlap two of the long edges by about 10cm/3¾in so that the pieces form a cushion back 43cm/17¼in square. Then place the cushion front on top (there is no right or wrong side to the front or the back pieces). Carefully pin the front to the backs around the outside edge, easing in the front to fit if necessary.
Join the seam with overcast stitches, or with double crochet.
Turn the cover right side out and insert the covered cushion.

filet cushion

Filet, from the French word for net, is basically two simple stitches — chain and treble — which are combined to create a square mesh, with some spaces in the mesh filled to form a motif or pattern. The simple lace look suits both traditional or contemporary interiors. A beautiful classic in pure white cotton, this cushion cover is very easy to make: the front is made up of nine squares of filet crochet joined together and finished with a picot edging to enhance its simplicity; the back is a piece of antique white linen.

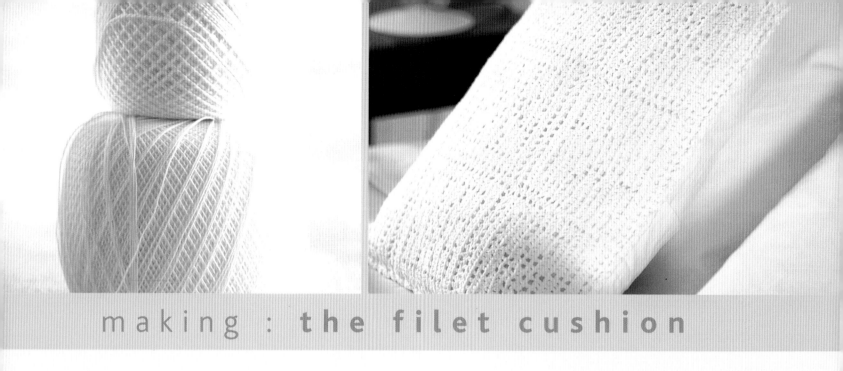

making : the filet cushion

CUSHION FRONT SIZE

Approximately 39cm/15³/4in square, excluding the picot edging.

MATERIALS

4 x 50g balls white Rowan *Siena 4ply* or a similar lightweight white cotton yarn (see page 122)
Hook size 3.50mm
Cushion pad 40cm/16in square
50cm/1yd of 112cm/44in wide white linen or cotton fabric and white sewing thread (see Tips)

STITCH SIZE

This cushion has a 'tension' (stitch size) of 13 spaces and 13 rows to 10cm/4in measured over filet crochet pattern. Each finished filet motif measures 13cm/5¹/4in square, but working to an exact tension is not essential (see Tips).

TECHNIQUES USED

Filet crochet, working with charts, joining motifs together and picot edge trimming.

TIPS

Tension

Don't worry about tension too much! If your cushion front ends up a bit bigger or smaller than the size given here, just adjust the size of the fabric cover to fit.

Joining in a new yarn

If your ball of yarn runs out while you are making one of the filet squares, join in a new one at the end of a row. Begin the last treble of the row in the usual way, but change to the new ball of yarn when drawing through the last loop of the stitch. Leave a long loose end of the old yarn and the new yarn to weave in later.

Buying a cushion pad

If you can't find a cushion pad the exact size you need, buy one that is slightly larger rather than slightly smaller so that it puffs up the cover nicely.

Fabric cushion cover

There are instructions for making your own fabric cushion cover, but if you like, you can buy a ready-made plain white covered cushion and stitch your crochet to it.

Filet crochet charts

Filet crochet instructions are usually charted. The blank squares on the chart represent 'spaces' in the filet and the squares with a symbol in them represent the solid 'blocks' of trebles. To follow a filet chart, read the odd-numbered rows from right to left and the even-numbered rows from left to right. From this basic filet technique many different patterns can be designed.

INSPIRATION

Experiment with different weights of yarn, colours and patterns to give a modern twist to the traditional. Use one motif as an insert in a linen bag or join three squares in a strip and use them as an edging on a velvet or satin pillowslip for a contemporary boudoir or guest room.

METHOD

Foundation chain Leaving a long loose end and using a 3.50mm hook, make 38 chain.

Row 1 Work 1tr into 6th chain from hook to make first 'space', *1ch, miss 1ch, 1tr into next ch, repeat from * to end. Turn. There are 17 'spaces' in the row.

Row 2 4ch to count as first tr and first 1-ch space, miss first tr and first 1-ch space, *1tr into next tr, 1tr into next 1-ch space (inserting hook *under* the chain – not *into* the chain – when working the tr), repeat from * to last tr, 1tr into last tr, 1ch, miss 1ch, 1tr into next ch (top of turning chain). Turn.

Row 3 4ch to count as first tr and first 1-ch space, miss first tr and first 1-ch space, 1tr into each of next 5tr (this makes one 'filet space' followed by 2 'filet blocks', [1ch, miss next tr, 1tr into next tr] 5 times (this makes 5 'spaces'), 1tr into each of next 2tr (this makes one 'block'), [1ch, miss next tr, 1tr into next tr] 5 times (this

makes 5 more 'spaces'), 1tr into each of next 4tr (this makes 2 'blocks'), 1ch, miss next ch, 1tr into next ch (this makes one last 'space'). Turn.

Row 4 4ch, miss first tr and first 1-ch space, 1tr into each of next 3tr, 1ch, miss 1tr, [1tr into next tr, 1tr into next 1-ch space] 3 times, 1tr into next tr, 1ch, miss next 1-ch space, 1tr into next tr, 1tr into next 1-ch space, 1tr into each of next 3tr, 1tr into next 1-ch space, 1tr into next tr, 1ch, miss next 1-ch space, [1tr into next tr, 1tr into next 1-ch space] 3 times, 1tr into next tr, 1ch, miss 1tr, 1tr into each of next 3tr, 1ch, miss next ch, 1tr into next ch. Turn.

Row 5 4ch, miss first tr, 1tr into each of next 3tr, [1ch, 1tr into each of next 7tr] 3 times, 1ch, 1tr into each of next 3tr, 1ch, miss next ch, 1tr into next ch. Turn.

Row 6 4ch, miss first tr, 1tr into each of next 3tr, 1ch, 1tr into each of next 7tr, 1tr into next 1-ch space, 1tr into next tr, 1ch, miss next tr, 1tr into each of next 3tr, 1ch, miss next tr, 1tr into next tr, 1tr into next 1-ch space, 1tr into each of next 7tr, 1ch, 1tr into each of next 3tr, 1ch, miss next ch, 1tr into next ch. Turn.

When working the next row, watch the chart as you make the 'spaces' and 'blocks' – you will see that each space on the chart is made up of a chain with a treble on each side and each block is made by working a treble where the chain would have been in the filet mesh. (See Tips for reading chart.)

Row 7 4ch, miss first tr, 1tr into each of next 3tr, 1ch, 1tr into next tr, [1ch, miss next tr, 1tr into next tr] twice, 1tr into each of next 4tr, 1ch, 1tr into next tr, 1ch,

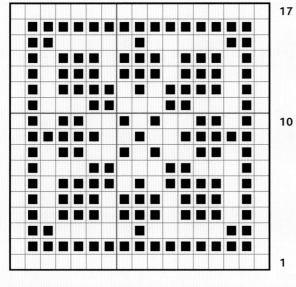

KEY

 = space

■ = block

miss next tr, 1tr into next tr, 1ch, 1tr into each of next 5tr, [1ch, miss next tr, 1tr into next tr] twice, 1ch, 1tr into each of next 3tr, 1ch, miss next ch, 1tr into next ch. Turn.

Continue forming the pattern with 'blocks' and 'spaces' in this way, and following the chart for the pattern, until row 17 has been completed. Fasten off. Work a total of 9 squares.

TO FINISH

Weave in any loose ends on the wrong side of the work.

Lay the nine pieces out flat, then steam and press lightly.

Oversew the squares together.

Picot edging

For a detailed finish, work a simple picot-stitch edging all around square. Begin by joining the yarn to a corner of the filet patchwork with a slip stitch. Then work the edging round and round the edge as follows:

Round 1 4ch to count as first tr and first 1-ch space, [1ch, 1tr] twice into same corner, then repeat [1ch, 1tr] evenly all around the edge, working the treble into each treble along the top and bottom, and into the top of each row end along the sides, and working [1ch, 1tr] 3 times into each of remaining three corners; at end of round, join with a slip stitch to 3rd of first 4-ch.

Round 2 1ch, 1dc into same place as slip stitch, 1dc into each 1-ch space (inserting hook *under* the chain – not *into* the chain – when working a dc into a 1-ch space) and 1dc into each dc to end of round; join with a slip stitch to first dc.

Round 3 1ch, 1dc into same place as slip stitch, 1dc into each dc to end of round; join with a slip stitch to first dc.

Round 4 1ch, [1dc, 5ch, 1dc] all into same place as slip stitch to form first *picot*, 1dc into next dc, *[1dc, 5ch, 1dc] all into next dc, 1dc into next dc, repeat from * to end; join with a slip stitch to first dc. Fasten off.

FABRIC COVER

Cut your piece of white fabric to 42cm/17in by 101cm/40 1/4 in. Begin the cover by making a hem along each of the two short edges. Fold 1.5cm/1/2 in, then 4cm/1 1/2 in to the wrong side and pin. Baste, then topstitch these two hems. Remove the basting and press. Lay the piece on a flat surface with the right side facing upwards. Fold each hemmed edge towards the centre and overlap them by 12cm/4 3/4 in so that the cover measures 39cm/15 3/4 in from fold to fold. Pin the open sides together and baste. Sew the seams 1.5cm/5/8 in from the raw edges. Trim the seams and finish the raw edges with a zigzag stitch. Remove the basting, turn right side out and press.

Hand-stitch the crochet piece to the front of the fabric cover, stitching around the edge of the filet-square patchwork and leaving the picot edging free.

t h r o w s

pieced throw

The effect of this throw is like a traditional 'strippy' patchwork, worked in

long strips that are then joined together. Each strip is in half treble crochet

in blocks of colour – natural ecru with brilliant shades of pink and orange.

The colours are staggered on each strip to produce a patchwork pattern.

After the strips are crocheted together, they are finished with an edging of

pink. As it is made in cotton, this throw is cool in summer and warm in winter.

Great for bedroom or sitting room, it can be laundered time after time.

making : the pieced throw

THROW SIZE

Approximately 107cm x 138cm/42³/4in x 56in, including edging.

MATERIALS

Rowan *Handknit DK Cotton* or a similar medium-weight yarn (see page 122) in 3 contrasting colours as follows:

Colour A: 8 x 50g balls pink
Colour B: 12 x 50g balls ecru
Colour C: 6 x 50g balls orange
Hook sizes 4.00mm and 4.50mm

STITCH SIZE

This throw has a stitch size of 14 stitches and 11¹/2rows to 10cm/4in measured over half treble crochet.

Each of the 10 strips of crochet is 13.5cm/5 ¹/2in wide by 104cm/41³/4in long, but working to an exact tension is not essential (see Tips).

TECHNIQUES USED

Half treble crochet, double crochet and joining in new balls of yarn.

TIPS

Tension

Don't worry about tension too much! Because this is a throw, an exact width is not that important and you can make it any length you want by adding to or subtracting from the number of rows worked.

Starting each strip

The foundation chain of each strip is worked with a larger hook, so that the starting edge is not too tight and so that it is easier to work the crochet edging into it.

Joining in a new yarn

This technique is used for changing yarns when your ball of yarn is finished or when you want to start a new colour for stripes. Change to the new yarn at the end of a row. Begin the last half treble in the usual way, by wrapping the yarn around the hook, inserting the hook into the 2-ch at the end of the row and drawing a loop through; then drop the old yarn/colour and draw the new yarn/colour through all 3 loops now on the hook to finish the half

treble crochet. Leave long loose ends of the old and new yarns to weave in later, or work over the ends for several stitches before clipping them off.

METHOD

Strip 1

Foundation chain Leaving a long loose end and using a 4.50mm hook and colour A (pink), make 20 chain.

Change to a 4.00mm hook and begin the half treble crochet as follows:

Row 1 Work 1htr into 3rd chain from hook, 1htr into each of remaining chain. Turn.

Row 2 2ch (this counts as first htr of row, so work it loosely), miss first htr and work 1htr into next htr, then work 1htr into each of remaining htr, work last htr into 2-ch at edge. Turn. There are 19 stitches in the row.

Repeating *row 2*, work 14 rows more in colour A (pink).

Continuing in htr throughout, work 16 rows B (ecru), 16 C (orange), 16 B (ecru),

16 A (pink), 16 B (ecru), 16 C (orange),
and 8 B (ecru). Fasten off.

The 9 following strips are worked in the
same stripe sequence, but started 8 rows
later in the sequence as follows:

Strip 2

Work as for strip 1, but change the stripe
sequence to 8 rows A (pink), 16 B (ecru),
16 C (orange), 16 B (ecru), 16 A (pink), 16
B (ecru), 16 C (orange), and 16 B (ecru).

Strip 3

Work as for strip 1, but change the stripe
sequence to16 rows B (ecru), 16 C (orange),
16 B (ecru), 16 A (pink), 16 B (ecru), 16 C
(orange), 16 B (ecru), and 8 A (pink).

Strip 4

Work as for strip 1, but change the stripe
sequence to 8 rows B (ecru), 16 C (orange),
16 B (ecru), 16 A (pink), 16 B (ecru), 16 C
(orange), 16 B (ecru), and 16 A (pink).

Strip 5

Work as for strip 1, but change the stripe
sequence to 16 rows C (orange), 16 B (ecru),
16 A (pink), 16 B (ecru), 16 C (orange), 16
B (ecru), 16 A (pink), and 8 B (ecru).

Strip 6

Work as for strip 1, but change the stripe
sequence to 8 rows C (orange), 16 B (ecru),
16 A (pink), 16 B (ecru), 16 C (orange), 16
B (ecru), 16 A (pink), and 16 B (ecru).

Strip 7

Work as for strip 1, but change the stripe
sequence to 16 rows B (ecru), 16 A (pink),
16 B (ecru), 16 C (orange), 16 B (ecru), 16
A (pink), 16 B (ecru), and 8 C (orange).

Strip 8

Work as for strip 1, but change the stripe
sequence to 8 rows B (ecru), 16 A (pink),
16 B (ecru), 16 C (orange), 16 B (ecru), 16
A (pink), 16 B (ecru), and 16 C (orange).

Strips 9 and 10

Work as for strips 1 and 2.

TO FINISH

Weave in any loose ends at the back of
the work.

Lay each strip out flat, then steam and
press lightly.

Arrange the bands side by side in the order
in which they were made (from right to
left), with all the foundation-chain edges
at the bottom. (Joined in this order, the
blocks of colours will form diagonal stripes
across the throw.) Join the strips together
by oversewing; or by holding the pieces
with right sides together and working a
row of dc in colour B (ecru) through both
thickness (1dc per row end).

Edging

Using a 4.00mm hook and colour A (pink),
work a row of double crochet around the
edge of the throw. For an even edging,
work 1dc into each chain along the
foundation-chain edge; 1dc into each dc
along the top; 1dc into each row end along
the sides; and 3dc into each corner to keep
the corners square.

Fasten off and weave in end.

textured throw

A timeless classic, this simple textured throw is an updated version of a traditional waffle blanket. It is worked in the simplest of textural stitches and bordered with a band of double crochet. Crocheted in a beautiful, matt, neutral, stone-coloured linen yarn, this throw is both sophisticated and modern. Use it anywhere – in the house, the garden or the car.

THROW SIZE

Approximately 123cm x 154cm/49¼in x 61¾in.

MATERIALS

29 x 50g balls Rowan *Cotton Glacé* or a similar lightweight cotton or linen yarn (see page 122)
Hook size 3.50mm

STITCH SIZE

This throw has a 'tension' (stitch size) of 6½ V-stitches and 8½ rows to 10cm/4in measured over V-stitch pattern, but working to an exact tension is not essential (see Tips).

TECHNIQUES USED

Treble crochet, working into a chain space, double crochet, working a border in rounds and joining in new balls of yarn.

TIPS

Tension and throw size
Don't worry about tension too much!

Because this is a throw, an exact size is not that important as long as it suits your purposes and the fabric is soft and supple. You can make the throw to any length you want by working more or fewer rows. You can also alter the width by adding to or subtracting from the number of V-stitches across the row. Make 3 foundation chain for every V-stitch you need – then work 3 extra foundation chain before starting *row 1*.

Joining in a new yarn
This technique is used for starting a new ball of yarn when the one you are using runs out or when working stripes. Begin your treble in the usual way, but change to the new ball of yarn when drawing through the last loop of the stitch. Leave a long loose end of the old yarn and the new yarn to weave in later.

INSPIRATION

Experiment with different yarn textures, such as lurex, suede or fine merino wool.

METHOD

Foundation chain Leaving a long loose end and using a 3.50mm hook, make 231 chain.
Row 1 Work 1tr into 4th chain from hook, 1ch, 1tr into next ch, *miss 1ch, 1tr into next ch, 1ch, 1tr into next chain, repeat from * to last ch, 1tr into last ch. Turn.
Row 2 Work 3ch to count as first tr, [1tr, 1ch, 1tr] into first 1-ch space (inserting hook *under* the chain – not *into* the chain – when working the trebles), *[1tr, 1ch, 1tr] into next 1-ch space, repeat from * to end, 1tr into top of turning chain. Turn. There are 76 V-stitches in the row. Repeat *row 2* until work measures 148cm/59¼in from foundation-chain edge (a total of about 126 rows from beginning). Fasten off.

TO FINISH

Weave any loose ends into the work. Lay the work out flat, then steam and press lightly.

Border

Using a 3.50mm hook, join yarn to edge of throw with a slip stitch by inserting hook through a chain near the centre of the foundation-chain edge of the throw and drawing a loop through, then work the border in rounds as follows:

Round 1 1ch, 1dc into same place as slip stitch was worked, 1dc into next ch, then continue in dc around the entire edge of the throw, working 1dc into each foundation chain, 2dc into each row end along the sides, 1dc into each stitch across the last row, and 3dc into each corner; join with a slip stitch to top of first dc of round.

Round 2 1ch, 1dc into same place as slip stitch was worked, then work 1dc into each dc along sides and 3dc into each centre dc of each 3dc-group at corners; join with a slip stitch to top of first dc of round. Work 5 rounds more as *round 2* for a 3cm/1¼in deep border.

Fasten off and weave in any remaining loose ends.

modern afghan

This is a simple, easy project to make and it can be picked up whenever time allows. Traditional crochet afghan squares are worked in subtle toning colours of soft natural cotton, joined together to make a stylish throw for sofa or car, or even the basket of your much-loved dog or cat. Cotton washes well time and time again, so it is not only comfortable but practical too. Each afghan square is worked in a combination of three of the colours, and they are joined together in a simple layout with the fourth colour. The blend of neutral colours chosen gives this little afghan a modern twist, but, if you wish, you can make it from leftover yarns from other projects in a vibrant mix of colours.

making : the modern afghan

AFGHAN SIZE

Approximately 75cm/29 1/2in square.
(This small size is for your dog – to make a bigger afghan, see Inspiration.)

MATERIALS

Rowan *Handknit DK Cotton* or a similar medium-weight cotton yarn (see page 122) in 4 contrasting colours as follows:

Colour A: 2 x 50g balls in off-white
Colour B: 2 x 50g balls in dark taupe
Colour C: 2 x 50g balls in black
Colour D: 3 x 50g balls in light beige
Hook size 3.00mm

STITCH SIZE

This afghan is made up of squares (made in 4 rounds) that measure 10cm/4in by 10cm/4in, but working to an exact 'tension' (stitch size) is not essential (see Tips).

TECHNIQUES USED

Working afghan squares in rounds, trebles, double crochet, joining squares together and working a simple border.

TIPS

Tension

Don't worry about tension too much! Because this is a throw, making it to an exact size is not important.

Working in rounds

When you work your crochet in rounds you never have to turn the fabric. The right side is always facing you.

Joining in new colours

When starting a new colour on your square motif, leave a long loose end of the old yarn and the new yarn to weave in later, or make less work for yourself by working over the yarn ends for several stitches before clipping them off.

Squares edgings

For a nice crisp edge on the motif squares, work the double crochet of the first round of the squares edging into the back loop of each stitch. Work the double crochet in *round 2* into both loops in the usual way.

Joining squares together

The easiest way to join the squares is given in the instructions, but if you are an experienced crocheter you can also join

them together with double crochet in the way patchwork blocks are joined. To do this, omit the squares edging and use colour D (light beige) to join the squares together into 6 strips of 6 squares. Work 4 rows of dc between the squares, joining them together on the 4th row with right sides facing. When you have joined squares into 6 strips, join the rows together in the same way, working 4 rows of dc between them and joining them together on the 4th row. Then work the outer border in 4 rounds of dc in colour D (light beige) and the final round in colour C (black).

INSPIRATION

Experiment with different colours, and try out different arrangements of the variously coloured squares. Use several colours or simply two colours, or make all the squares in a single colour for a simple but contemporary look. Vary the size of the afghan to suit your personal requirements – work larger squares or more of them to make a larger throw for the lounge or bedroom or car.

METHOD

The afghan is made up of 36 squares that are each worked in the round using 3 colours – A (off-white), B (dark taupe) and C (black). Work the first square as follows:

Foundation-chain ring Leaving a long loose end and using a 3.00mm hook and colour A, make 6 chain and join length of chain into a ring by working a slip stitch into first chain made.

Round 1 (right side) Using A, 3ch, 2tr into ring, *3ch, 3tr into ring, repeat from * twice more, 3ch; join with a slip stitch to 3rd of first 3-ch.
Break off colour A and fasten off.

Round 2 Using B, join on yarn with a slip stitch by inserting hook into any 3-ch space and drawing a loop through, 3ch, [2tr, 3ch, 3tr] into same space as slip stitch was worked, *1ch, [3tr, 3ch, 3tr] into next 3-ch space, repeat from * twice more, 1ch; join with a slip stitch to 3rd of first 3-ch.
Break off colour B and fasten off.

Round 3 Using C, join on yarn with a slip stitch by inserting hook into a 3-ch space and drawing a loop through, 3ch, [2tr, 3ch, 3tr] into same space as slip stitch was worked, *1ch, 3tr into next 1-ch space, 1ch, [3tr, 3ch, 3tr] into next 3-ch space, repeat from * twice more, 1ch, 3tr into next 1-ch space, 1ch; join with a slip stitch to 3rd of first 3-ch.
Break off colour C and fasten off.

Round 4 Using A, join on yarn with a slip stitch by inserting hook into a 3-ch space and drawing a loop through, 3ch, [2tr, 3ch, 3tr] into same space as slip stitch was worked, *[1ch, 3tr into next 1-ch space] twice, 1ch, [3tr, 3ch, 3tr] into next 3-ch space, repeat from * twice more, [1ch, 3tr into next 1-ch space] twice, 1ch; join with a slip stitch to 3rd of first 3-ch.
Fasten off.
Make 5 more squares exactly the same.
For the remaining 30 squares, vary the colour sequence as follows:
Make 6 squares – round 1 colour A; round 2 colour C; round 3 colour B; and round 4 colour A.
Make 6 squares – round 1 colour B; round 2 colour A; round 3 colour C; and round 4 colour B.
Make 6 squares – round 1 colour B; round 2 colour C; round 3 colour A; and round 4 colour B.
Make 6 squares – round 1 colour C; round 2 colour A; round 3 colour B; and round 4 colour C.
Make 6 squares – round 1 colour C; round 2 colour B; round 3 colour A; and round 4 colour C.

TO FINISH

Weave any loose ends into the work.

Squares edging
Using a 3.00mm hook and colour D (light beige), edge each square with 2 rounds of double crochet as follows:

Round 1 (right side) Join on yarn with a slip stitch by inserting hook into first chain of a 3-ch group at a corner and drawing a loop through, 1ch, 1dc into same place as slip stitch was worked, 3dc into next ch (corner chain), 1dc into next ch, [1dc into each of next 3tr, 1dc into next 1-ch] 3 times, 1dc into each of next 3tr, *1dc into first ch of next 3-ch group, 3dc into next ch, 1dc into next chain, [1dc into each of next 3tr, 1dc into next 1-ch] 3 times, 1dc into each of next 3tr, repeat from * twice more; join with a slip stitch to top of first dc.

Round 2 1ch, 1dc into same place as slip stitch was worked, 1dc into each dc along the sides and 3dc into each corner dc (the centre dc of each 3-dc group); join with a slip stitch to top of first dc.
Fasten off.

Joining squares
Arrange motifs into 6 rows of 6 squares so you have a good random mixture of the various colourways. Oversew the squares together into 6 strips of 6 squares, then oversew the strips together.
Lay the work out flat, then steam and press lightly.

Outer border
Using a 3.00mm hook, work 3 rounds of double crochet around the outer edge of the afghan as follows:

Round 1 (right side) Using D (light beige), join on yarn with a slip stitch by inserting hook into a dc along one edge of afghan and drawing a loop through, 1ch, 1dc into same place as slip stitch was worked, 1dc into each dc along the sides and 3dc into each corner dc (the centre dc of each 3-dc group); join with a slip stitch to top of first dc.

Round 2 Still using D, 1ch, 1dc into same place as slip stitch was worked, 1dc into each dc along the sides and 3dc into each corner dc (the centre dc of each 3-dc group); join with a slip stitch to top of first dc.

Round 3 Using C (black), work as round 2.
Fasten off.
Weave in any remaining loose ends.

stripy throw

Make this elegant throw for the sofa or for the car. It is worked in warm neutral colours with a beautiful cotton microfibre yarn that is lightweight and modern. The stitch pattern is a supple variation on basic double crochet and looks very effective in this simple repeating stripe pattern. The throw takes no time at all to crochet. It is lighter to work than knitting can be, so it's easy to pick up and put down.

making : **the stripy throw**

THROW SIZE
Approximately 83cm x 138cm/33in x 55in.

MATERIALS
Rowan *All Seasons Cotton* or a similar
medium-weight cotton yarn (see page
122) in 4 contrasting colours as follows:
Colour A: 10 x 50g balls in brown
Colour B: 5 x 50g balls in beige
Colour C: 3 x 50g balls in lime
Colour D: 2 x 50g balls in white
Hook size 6.00mm

STITCH SIZE
This throw has a 'tension' (stitch size) of
15 stitches and 14¹/₂ rows to 10cm/4in

measured over stitch pattern, but
working to an exact tension is not
essential (see Tips).

TECHNIQUES USED
Double crochet, working into a chain
space and joining in new balls of yarn.

TIPS
Tension
Don't worry about tension too much!
Because this is a throw, an exact width
is not that important and you can
make it any length you want by adding
to or subtracting from the number of
rows worked.

Joining in a new yarn
This technique is used for changing yarns
when your ball of yarn is finished or when
you want to start a new colour for stripes.
Change to the new yarn at the end of a
row. Begin the last double crochet in the
usual way, by drawing a loop through the
last chain space, then drop the old yarn
and draw the new yarn through both loops
now on the hook to finish the double
crochet (see Crochet Basics for
instructions on how to join in new yarn).
Leave long loose ends of the old and new
yarns to weave in later, or work over the
ends for several stitches before clipping
them off.

inspiration

If you wish, you can make a single-colour version of this throw, which exposes the simple textural beauty of the stitch. Alternatively, you can give your throw a completely different look by changing the colour scheme. Use varying shades of the same colour for a smoothly blending effect, or starkly contrasting tones for a striking boldness. Broader or narrower stripes, or wide uniform bands of colour, will also alter the effect. Before starting an original version, make a long thin strip to test your stripe creation.

METHOD

Foundation chain Leaving a long loose end and using a 6.00mm hook and colour A (brown), make 126 chain.

Row 1 Work 1dc into 4th chain from hook, *1ch, miss 1ch, 1dc into next ch, repeat from * to end. Turn.

Row 2 Make 2ch (this counts as first dc and first 1-ch space), miss first dc and work 1dc into first 1-ch space (inserting hook *under* the chain – not *into* the chain – when working the dc), *1ch, miss next dc, 1dc into next 1-ch space, repeat from * to end, working last dc into chain space at edge. Turn.

Repeating *row 2*, work 22 rows more in

pattern in colour A (brown).

Stripe pattern repeat

Continuing to repeat *row 2* for stitch pattern, work next 42 rows in stripes as follows:

Colour B (beige): 2 rows.
Colour A (brown): 2 rows.
Colour B (beige): 4 rows.
Colour C (lime): 2 rows.
Colour D (white): 2 rows.
Colour C (lime): 2 rows.
Colour D (white): 2 rows.
Colour C (lime): 2 rows.
Colour B (beige): 4 rows.
Colour A (brown): 2 rows.
Colour B (beige): 2 rows.

Colour A (brown): 16 rows.
Work this 42-row stripe-pattern repeat 4 times in total.
Work 8 rows more in A (brown), so that the throw ends with 24 rows A to match brown border at beginning.
Fasten off.

TO FINISH

Weave any loose ends into the work. Lay the work out flat, then steam and press lightly.

rag rug

This crocheted rag rug was created with simple natural linens and cottons in plain natural tones and in simple black and white patterns, including a ticking stripe and a gingham. You can make your own rug from scraps, recycled from worn-out or outgrown clothes, or various remnants. The fabric is simply cut up into thin strips of various lengths and crocheted together randomly with a large hook. Rag rugs work well in hallways or bathrooms, on flagstones or parquet. The ends of the rag strips can be woven into the crochet or knotted and left sticking out for a textured effect.

making : the rag rug

RAG RUG SIZE
Approximately 66.5cm x 87.5cm/26 1/2in x 35in.

MATERIALS
Scraps of an assortment of fabric (the rug shown here was made from cotton/linen mixes in three natural shades, a black linen, a white linen, a cotton ticking with narrow black and white stripes, a black and white gingham, and a black and white check)
Hook size 8.00mm

STITCH SIZE
This rug has a 'tension' (stitch size) of 7 1/2 stitches and 8 rows to 10cm/4in measured over double crochet, but working to an exact tension is not essential (see Tips for more about tension).

TECHNIQUES USED
Making yarns from fabric by cutting into strips, double crochet and joining in new fabric strips.

TIPS
Tension
Don't worry about tension too much! Because this rug can be made to any size and is worked randomly, it doesn't matter what your tension is as long as it produces a nice soft rug. If your stitches are so tight you find them difficult to work comfortably, try a larger hook size.
Cutting fabric strips
Before starting to crochet, cut some long strips from each of your fabrics. Make the strips about 1.5cm/5/8in wide and cut them on the straight grain of the fabric. If you like, you can roll the strips into balls

just like balls of ordinary yarn. When you run out of strips as you are crocheting, cut more as you need them.
Joining in a new strip
This technique is used for starting a new strip when the one you are using runs out or when changing to a new colour for stripes. Begin a double crochet in the usual way, by drawing a loop through the next stitch, then drop the old strip and draw the new strip through both loops now on the hook to finish the double crochet (see Crochet Basics). Leave long loose ends of the old and new strips to weave in later, or work over the ends for several stitches before clipping them off.

METHOD
Foundation chain Leaving a long loose end and using an 8.00mm hook and a plain

inspiration

Experiment with different fabric textures, but try to keep the strips to a similar width when cutting. Use different colour tones or work regular stripes instead of random ones. Vary the size of the rug to suit your personal requirements — maybe a runner for a hallway — or work manageable sections or squares and sew them together to make a larger rug for the lounge or bedroom. Use fabric strips in patterns, prints and stripes of similar tones to create special effects. Try working in a spiral (as for the round cushion cover on pages 30–33) to create a circular rug.

natural-coloured fabric strip, make 50 chain.

Row 1 Work 1dc into 2nd chain from hook, 1dc into each of remaining chain. Turn.

Joining in new strips of fabric at random for a random stripe effect, continue as follows:

Row 2 1ch (this counts as first dc of row, so work it loosely), miss first dc and work 1dc into next dc, then work 1dc into each of remaining dc, work last dc into 1-ch at edge. Turn. There are 50 stitches in the row.

Repeat *row 2* until rug measures approximately 87.5cm/35in from foundation-chain edge (a total of about 70 rows from beginning) or to the desired length.

Fasten off.

TO FINISH

Weave any loose ends into the double crochet. Lay the work out flat, then steam and press lightly.

containers

boxes

These simple crocheted boxes have a variety of uses – to store shoes or jewellery, to stack cutlery in, or to display yarns and threads for projects; or put them to use in the bathroom. Have fun thinking up new combinations of colours and textures, and give the boxes as a gift, attractive and useful. They are worked in basic double crochet using parcel string, trimmed with cotton 'rag' strips. Three different shapes and sizes are given here, but it is very easy to make them to suit your own requirements.

making : the boxes

BOX SIZES

Box A: The tall square box with orange trim measures 15cm x 15cm x 20.5cm tall/6in x 6in x 8^{1}/$_{4}$in tall.

Box B: The small rectangular box with bright pink trim measures 27cm x 10.5cm x 8cm tall/10^{3}/$_{4}$in x 4^{1}/$_{4}$in x 3^{1}/$_{4}$in tall.

Box C: The large rectangular box with pale pink trim measures 29.5cm x 21cm x 12cm tall/11^{3}/$_{4}$in x 8^{1}/$_{4}$in x 4^{3}/$_{4}$in tall.

Note that the instructions are given for box A (the square box) and the figures for the two rectangular boxes are given in parentheses like this – box A (box B: box C).

MATERIALS

4(2:5) x 40m/44yd balls thick parcel string (available from local hardware stores or stationers)
Fabric remnants for rag edging – in orange, bright pink and pale pink
Hook sizes 4.50mm and 5.00mm

STITCH SIZE

These boxes have a 'tension' (stitch size) of 11^{1}/$_{2}$ stitches and 13 rows to 10cm/4in measured over double crochet, but working to an exact tension is not essential (see Tips).

TECHNIQUES USED

Double crochet, joining in new balls of yarn and making yarn from fabric by cutting into strips.

TIPS

Tension

Don't worry about tension too much! Because the boxes can be made to any size, it doesn't matter what your tension is as long as it produces a fairly stiff fabric that will hold its shape nicely. Just make the sides and ends of the boxes first, following the instructions given. Then make the base, adding to or subtracting from the number of rows recommended until the depth of the piece matches the width of the ends.

Joining in a new yarn

This technique is used for starting a new ball of yarn when the one you are using runs out. Begin a double crochet in the usual way, by drawing a loop through the next stitch, then drop the old yarn and draw the new yarn through both loops now on the hook to finish the double crochet (see Crochet Basics). Leave a long loose end of the old and new yarns to weave in later, or work over the ends before clipping them off.

Cutting fabric strips

For the rag edging on the boxes, cut some long fabric strips about 1.5cm/^{5}/$_{8}$in wide and cut them on the straight grain of the fabric. If you like, you can roll the strips into balls just like balls of ordinary yarn. For a long continuous strip, cut along the first edge, then turn at the corner, cutting in a spiral towards the centre.

String is a good material for crochet boxes, but you could also try using other textures and colours, or make a whole box with rag strips in various shades and in prints, stripes and patterns. Just work the double crochet tightly to keep the fabric firm. Use the boxes for storage – the ones here create an attractive display on the bathroom shelf.

METHOD

Box sides (make 2)

Foundation chain Leaving a long loose end and using a 5.00mm hook and string, make 17(31:34) chain.

Row 1 Work 1dc into 2nd chain from hook, 1dc into each of remaining chain. Turn.

Row 2 1ch (this counts as first dc of row, so work it loosely), miss first dc and work 1dc into next dc, then work 1dc into each of remaining dc, work last dc into 1-ch at edge. Turn. There are 17(31:34) stitches in the row.

Repeat *row 2* until work measures 19(6.5:10.5)cm/7³⁄₄(2³⁄₄:4¹⁄₄)in from foundation-chain edge – a total of about 25(9:14) rows from beginning.

Fasten off.

Box ends (make 2)

Foundation chain Leaving a long loose end and using a 5.00mm hook and string, make 17(12:24) chain.

Work *rows 1* and *2* as for box sides.

Repeat *row 2* on these 17(12:24) stitches until there are same number of rows as on sides.

Fasten off.

Box base (make 1)

Foundation chain Leaving a long loose end and using a 5.00mm hook and string, make 17(31:34) chain.

Work *rows 1* and *2* as for box sides.

Repeat *row 2* on these 17(31:34) stitches until work measures 15(10.5:21)cm/ 6(4¹⁄₄:8¹⁄₄)in from foundation-chain edge – a total of about 19(14:27) rows from beginning.

Fasten off.

TO FINISH

Weave any loose ends into work.

Oversew the ends and sides together along the short seams to make a box shape – the seams are meant to show on the outside of the box, so hold the pieces with the wrong sides together when seaming.

Oversew the box base to the sides and ends in the same way.

'Rag' edging

Using a 4.50mm hook and string, work a row of dc all around the top of the box.

Fasten off.

Using a 4.50mm hook and a orange (bright pink: pale pink) fabric strip (see Tips), work another row of dc.

Fasten off. Sew in any loose ends.

string bottle cover

These sculptural containers have a strong architectural presence. Created in natural yarns – a combination of hemp and simple string – they are worked in basic double crochet. The covers have been designed to fit neatly over wine or mineral water bottles as decoration. Equally, an empty bottle can be used as a vase.

BOTTLE COVER SIZE

Approximately 45cm/17 3/4in tall.
See Tips for adjusting circumference to fit different bottle sizes.

MATERIALS

1 x large ball medium-weight brown string; and 2 x 40m/44yd balls thick natural-coloured parcel string (both available from local hardware stores or stationers)
Hook size 5.50mm
Wine or water bottle
Two lengths of contrasting coloured yarn or two safety pins for markers

STITCH SIZE

This bottle cover has a 'tension' (stitch size) of 10 1/2 stitches and 11 1/2 rows to 10cm/4in measured over double crochet using one strand of thick string or 2 strands of medium-weight brown string,

but working to an exact tension is not essential (see Tips).

TECHNIQUES USED

Double crochet, working in rounds, simple decreases and joining in new balls of yarn.

TIPS

Working in rounds

When you work your crochet in rounds you never have to turn the fabric. The right side is always facing you.

Bottle size and tension

Don't worry about tension too much! A cover worked to the specified stitch size will easily fit a standard-size wine bottle or a big mineral-water bottle with plenty of room to spare, and the circumference of the cover is easy to alter. Work the first 3 rounds of the cover, then slip it over your bottle – it should slide on easily,

with room left over. If you want a slightly snugger fit or if the cover it too tight, just start over, making the foundation chain a little shorter or a little longer.

Joining in a new yarn

This technique is used for changing yarns when your ball of yarn is finished or when you want to start a new colour for stripes. Begin a double crochet in the usual way, by drawing a loop through the next stitch, then drop the old yarn and draw the new yarn through both loops now on the hook to finish the double crochet. Leave a long loose end of the old and new yarns to weave in later, or work over the ends for several stitches before clipping them off.

METHOD

Foundation-chain ring Leaving a long loose end and using a 5.50mm hook and 2 strands of medium-weight brown string

inspiration

Try using different string textures or different stripe combinations for your bottle covers. To make round baskets to go with your bottle covers, first work the circular bottom of the container following the instructions for the round string cushion on pages 30–33. When the circle is the diameter required for your basket, stop adding stitches. If you continue on this fixed number of stitches, the sides of the basket will begin to form. Fasten off when the basket is the desired height.

together, make 33 chain and join length of chain into a ring by working a slip stitch into first chain made.

Round 1 (right side) Make 1 chain, work 1dc into same chain as slip stitch was worked, 1dc into each of remaining 32ch. There are now 33dc in the round.

Round 2 (right side) Miss the slip stitch and the 1-ch and work 1dc into top of first dc of previous round, 1dc into each of the remaining 32dc of previous round. 33dc. Continue working these 33 stitches in rounds in a spiral until work measures 13cm/5in from foundation-chain edge. Change to one strand of thick parcel string and continue until work measures 23cm/9in from foundation-chain edge. (As the cover is being worked in a spiral there is no need to keep track of exactly where each new round begins and ends, so when the cover is 23cm/9in tall you can start

the next round in any place you choose.) Decrease 2 stitches in next round as follows:

Next round (decrease round) [Insert hook into next dc, yarn round hook and draw a loop through] twice, yarn round hook and draw through all 3 loops on hook—called *decrease one stitch*—, mark the decrease just made with a coloured thread or a safety pin, continue in dc until half way around work from first decrease, then *decrease one stitch*, mark the decrease just made, 1dc into each of remaining dc of round. 31dc.

Work one round without decreasing. Work 2 decreases evenly spaced on next round and on 2 following alternate rounds, working decreases as before and positioning them roughly above the marked decreases on the first decrease round. 25dc.

Continue in dc without shaping until work measures 32cm/12 1/2in. Decrease 2 stitches as before on next round and 3 following alternate rounds. 17dc.

Work in dc until work measures 45cm/ 17 3/4in.

Work a slip stitch into each of next few dc to taper the stitch height and neaten the edge. Fasten off.

TO FINISH

Weave the loose ends into the wrong side of the cover.

log basket

For the ultimate in crochet, make a fireside
basket in rich black leather, or sisal, string
or hemp and use it for logs, newspapers,
magazines or general clutter. Crocheting
with leather thonging takes a little dexterity
and patience, but the results are stunning.
Worked in double crochet with a really large
hook, the basket is made in five pieces that
are then sewn together. Large 'buttonholes'
serve as handles. Work to dimensions that
suit your budget and purpose.

BASKET SIZE

Approximately 37.5cm x 30cm x 25cm tall/15in x 12in x 10in tall.

MATERIALS

9 x 50m/55yd balls 2mm-thick round leather thonging (available from craft stores or leather merchants); or sisal or hemp string
Hook sizes 9.00mm, 8.00mm and 7.00mm
Large upholstery sewing needle – optional (see Tips)

STITCH SIZE

This basket has a 'tension' (stitch size) of 8 stitches and 10 rows to 10cm/4in measured over double crochet, but working to an exact tension is not essential (see Tips).

TECHNIQUES USED

Double crochet and joining in new balls of yarn.

TIPS

Tension and basket size

Don't worry about tension too much! As the basket can be made to any size, it doesn't matter what your tension is as long as it produces a fairly stiff fabric that will hold its shape nicely. Just make the sides and ends of the basket following the instructions given. Then make the base, adding to or subtracting from the number of rows recommended until the depth of the piece matches the width of the ends. If you wish to achieve a particular size, do a small square to test your stitch size, then calculate the number of rows and stitches you'll need (see page 17).

Joining in a new yarn

This technique is used for starting a new ball of yarn when the one you are using runs out. Begin a double crochet in the usual way, by drawing a loop through the next stitch, then drop the old yarn and draw the new yarn through both loops now on the hook to finish the double crochet (see Crochet Basics for how to work double crochet). Leave a long loose end of the old and new yarns to weave in later, or work over the ends for several stitches before clipping them off.

Leather

Leather is quite hard on the hands, so concentrate on one stitch at a time, as a unique aspect of constructing a special textile. Warm the leather in your hands as you work to soften it. It can be a little sticky, too, and a little talcum powder on the hook may assist to pull it through.

Sewing together

To sew the leather basket pieces together, use a large upholstery needle. Alternatively, you can simply weave the end of the thonging directly through the crochet fabric, as it is rigid enough to do this.

INSPIRATION

Experiment with different yarn textures, sisal string or hemp. Make the basket in a texture of your choice and fill with supplies for a new home or baby, as a personal gift or to co-ordinate with the décor of a room.

METHOD

Basket sides (make 2)

Foundation chain Leaving a long loose end and using a 9.00mm hook and leather thonging, make 30 chain.

Change to an 8.00mm hook and begin working in double crochet as follows:

Row 1 Work 1dc into 2nd chain from hook, 1dc into each of remaining chain. Turn.

Row 2 1ch (this counts as first dc of row, so work it loosely), miss first dc and work 1dc into next dc, then work 1dc into each of remaining dc, work last dc into 1-ch at edge. Turn. There are 30 stitches in the row.

Repeat *row 2* until work measures 17cm/6 3/4in from foundation-chain edge – a total of about 17 rows from beginning.

'Buttonhole'/slot for handle

Start making the slot for the handle on the next row as follows:

Next row 1ch (to count as first dc), miss first dc and work 1dc into next dc, then work 1dc into each of next 7dc. Turn. There are now 9 stitches in this short row.

Next row 1ch, miss first dc and work 1dc into next dc, then work 1dc into each of next 6dc, work last dc into 1-ch at edge. Turn.

Leave the thonging where it is now – at the outside edge of the piece – but do not cut it off as you will return to it after working the other side of the slot.

Second side of slot

Using a new ball of thonging and with the piece facing you so that the short rows just worked are on the right, miss the first 12 stitches of the section left unworked and insert the hook through the next dc, yarn round hook and draw a loop through, 1ch, miss next dc and work 1dc into next dc, 1dc into each of next 6dc, work last dc into 1-ch at edge. Turn. There are 9 stitches in this short row.

Next row 1ch, miss first dc and work 1dc into next dc, then work 1dc into each of next 6dc, work last dc into 1-ch at edge. Fasten off.

Join sides of slot

Return to first side of handle 'buttonhole', pick up thonging left at outside edge and continue as follows:

Next row 1ch, miss first dc and work 1dc into next dc, then work 1dc into each of next 6dc, 1dc into 1-ch at handle edge, then make 12 chain over the gap, 1dc into each of next 8dc on second side of handle, work last dc into 1-ch at edge. Turn.

Next row 1ch, miss first dc and work 1dc into next dc, 1dc into each of next 7dc, 1dc into each chain, 1dc into each of next 8dc, work last dc into 1-ch at edge. Turn. There are now 30 stitches in the row.

Now continue in dc until side measures 24cm/9 1/2in from foundation-chain edge – a total of about 24 rows from beginning. Fasten off.

Basket ends (make 2)

Foundation chain Leaving a long loose end and using a 9.00mm hook and leather thonging, make 24 chain.

Change to an 8.00mm hook and work *rows 1* and *2* as for basket sides.

Repeat *row 2* on these 24 stitches until there are same number of rows as on sides. Fasten off.

Basket base (make 1)

Foundation chain Leaving a long loose end and using a 9.00mm hook and leather thonging, make 30 chain.

Change to an 8.00mm hook and work *rows 1* and *2* as for basket sides.

Repeat *row 2* on these 30 stitches until work measures 30cm/12in from foundation-chain edge (check that it is deep enough to fit ends and adjust if necessary).

Fasten off.

TO FINISH

Weave in all loose ends, taking care not to cut them off too short.

Join the ends and sides by oversewing with wrong sides together and pushing thonging through row ends or using a large upholstery needle (see Tips).

Attach base either by oversewing, or by working dc through both layers with a 7.00mm hook, so that the seam is on the outside.

Finally, to firm up the top edge of the basket, work a row of dc all around the top using a 7.00mm hook.

Fasten off and weave in any remaining loose ends.

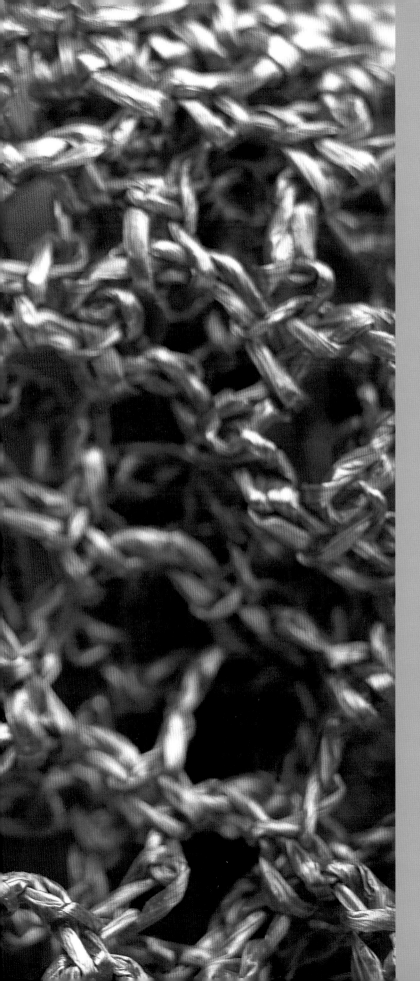

string bag

Made with coloured plastic string, available in hardware stores or stationery shops, this string bag is very inexpensive to make and easy to work. Make several in different colours, filled with colourful plastic toys, to hang next to the nursery bathtub. Alternatively, hang them in the pantry, and fill them with fruit and vegetables. Work alternatives in natural string or leather thonging, fill with seashells and driftwood, and hang them in the bathroom.

making : the string bag

BAG SIZE
Approximately 33cm/13in deep, but the bag is very stretchy.

MATERIALS
2 x 89m/98yd balls coloured multipurpose polypropylene string (available from local hardware stores or stationers)
Hook size 4.00mm
Length of contrasting coloured yarn for marker

STITCH SIZE
This bag has a 'tension' (stitch size) of 5 5-chain loops to 10cm/4in measured over crochet stitch used for bag, but working to an exact tension is not essential (see Tips).

TECHNIQUES USED
Double crochet, working in rounds, working into chain spaces and joining in new balls of yarn.

TIPS
Tension
Don't worry about tension too much! Because this is a string bag, you needn't work it to an exact size, and as it is worked round and round in a spiral, you can just keep working until the bag is the required size.
Working in rounds
When you work your crochet in rounds you never have to turn the fabric. The same side is always facing you.
Marking the beginning of a round
Be sure to mark the beginning of each round to make it easier to keep your place.
Joining in a new yarn
This technique is used for changing yarns when your ball of yarn is finished. Begin a double crochet in the usual way, by drawing a loop through the next stitch, then drop the old yarn and draw the new yarn through both loops now on the hook

to finish the double crochet (see Crochet Basics). Leave a long loose end of the old yarn to weave in later.

METHOD
Foundation-chain ring Leaving a long loose end and using a 4.00mm hook, make 4 chain and join length of chain into a ring by working a slip stitch into first chain made.

Round 1 Make 1 chain, work 8dc into ring, working over long loose end. Before starting the next round, place a short length of a contrasting yarn across your crochet fabric from front to back, tight up against the loop on the hook and above the working yarn. Then start to work the double crochet of *round 2*, catching the marker in position. The marker will show you where the round started, as it will be caught under the top of the first stitch of the round.

Round 2 *1ch, 1dc into next dc, repeat from * to end, making sure you are no longer working over loose end.
At the end of each round pull the marker out and place it across your crochet, up against the loop on the hook as before, so it will always be under the top of the first stitch of the round showing you where to start the next round.

Round 3 *2ch, 1dc into next 1-ch space, repeat from * to end.

Round 4 *3ch, 1dc into next 2-ch space, repeat from * to end. There are now 8 3-ch spaces in the round.

Round 5 *[3ch, 1dc] twice into next 3-ch space, repeat from * to end. 16 3-ch spaces.

Rounds 6, 7 and 8 *3ch, 1dc into next 3-ch space, repeat from * to end.

Round 9 *5ch, 1dc into next 3-ch space, repeat from * to end.

Round 10 *[5ch, 1dc] twice into next 5-ch space, 5ch, 1dc into next 5-ch space, repeat from * to end. 24 5-ch spaces.

Round 11 *5ch, 1dc into next 5-ch space, repeat from * to end.

Rounds 12–14 Work 3 rounds as round 11.

Round 15 As round 10. 36 5-ch spaces.

Rounds 16–21 Work 6 rounds as round 11.

Round 22 *4ch, 1dc into next 5-ch space, repeat from * to end.

Round 23 *3ch, 1dc into next 4-ch space, repeat from * to end.

Round 24 *2ch, 1dc into next ch space, repeat from * to end.

Round 25 As round 24.

Round 26 *1dc into next dc, 2dc into next 2-ch space, repeat from * to end. 108dc.

Handles

Rounds 27 and 28 1dc into each of next 33dc, 52ch, miss next 21dc, 1dc into each of next 33dc, 52ch, miss next 21dc; now work 1dc into each dc and 1dc into each chain around top of bag and handles. Slip stitch into next dc and fasten off.

TO FINISH
Pull the long loose end at the centre of the circle to tighten up the hole and weave it into the work. Weave in any other loose ends as well.

at home

turkish slippers

These stylish slippers were inspired by little Turkish shoes. They are worked in double crochet in a medium-weight cotton yarn, used double, so they don't take long to make. Each slipper is worked in one piece, then the heel seam is joined at the back. For comfort, the sole is best lined with a ready-made insole. A simple felt lining in a toning colour covers the insole.

SLIPPER SIZE

Approximately 24(27)cm/9$\frac{1}{2}$(10$\frac{1}{2}$)in in length.

The pattern is written for two women's sizes, but is adjustable to suit your specific size.

MATERIALS

4(4) x 50g balls Rowan *Handknit DK Cotton* or a similar medium-weight yarn (see page 122)

Hook sizes 4.00mm and 5.00mm

Length of contrasting yarn for marker

Large blunt-ended needle

Pair of ready-made insoles

Contrasting or toning coloured felt to cover top of insole

Fabric glue

STITCH SIZE

These slippers have a 'tension' (stitch size) of 12$\frac{1}{2}$ stitches and 14 rows to 10cm/4in measured over double crochet, using the yarn double.

TECHNIQUES USED

Double crochet, working in rounds, simple increases and joining in new balls of yarn.

TIPS

Tension

Make a swatch of double crochet to test your stitch size. If you are getting more than 12$\frac{1}{2}$ stitches to 10cm/4in, try a larger hook size; less than 12$\frac{1}{2}$ stitches, a smaller hook. Don't worry too much about the number of rows to 10cm/4in as you can easily adjust the length.

Working in rounds

When you work your crochet in rounds you never have to turn the fabric. The right side is always facing you.

Marking the beginning of a round

Be sure to mark the beginning of each round to make it easier to keep your place.

Joining in a new yarn

This technique is used for changing yarns when your ball of yarn is finished or when you want to start a new colour for stripes. Begin a double crochet in the usual way, by drawing a loop through the next stitch, then drop the old yarn and draw the new yarn through both loops now on the hook to finish the double crochet. Leave a long loose end of the old and new yarns to weave in later, or work over the ends for several stitches before clipping them off.

Joining the seam

Leave a long loose end when fastening off the crochet after the last row of the slipper. You can use this length for sewing the back heel seam.

INSPIRATION

Experiment with different yarn textures, heavier or finer yarns, or try regular-colour or random-colour stripes. Instead of felt, use a floral or stripe print to cover the insole, or you may wish to edge the slipper opening with a contrast or toning colour yarn or fabric.

METHOD

Foundation-chain ring Leaving a long loose end and using a 5.00mm hook and 2 strands of yarn together, make 4 chain and join the length of chain into a ring by working a slip stitch into first chain made.

Round 1 (right side) Make 1 chain, work 6dc into ring, working over the long loose end; join with a slip stitch to top of first dc of round.

Round 2 (right side) 1ch, place a short length of a contrasting yarn across your crochet fabric from front to back, tight up against the loop on the hook and above the working yarn—called *place marker*—, 2dc into same place as slip stitch was worked, 2dc into each of remaining 5dc of round; join with a slip stitch to first dc of round (ignore slip stitch and 1-ch and work into top of first dc – your marker marks the spot). There are now 12dc in the round.

Round 3 1ch, pull marker out of previous round and place marker as before, 1dc into same place as slip stitch, 1dc into each dc to end; join with a slip stitch to first dc. Continue to pull out your marker and place it after working the first chain of each round.

Round 4 1ch, 1dc into same place as slip stitch, 2dc into the next dc, *1dc into next dc, 2dc into next dc, repeat from * to end; join with a slip stitch to first dc. 18dc.

Round 5 As round 3.

Round 6 1ch, 1dc into same place as slip stitch, 1dc into each of next 4dc, 2dc into next dc, *1dc into each of next 5dc, 2dc into next dc, repeat from * to end; join with a slip stitch to first dc. 21dc.

Round 7 As round 3.

Round 8 1ch, 1dc into same place as slip stitch, 1dc into each of next 5dc, 2dc into next dc, *1dc into each of next 6dc, 2dc into next dc, repeat from * to end; join with a slip stitch to first dc. 24dc.

Round 9 As round 3.

Round 10 1ch, 1dc into same place as slip stitch, 1dc into each of next 6dc, 2dc into next dc, *1dc into each of next 7dc, 2dc into next dc, repeat from * to end; join with a slip stitch to first dc. 27dc.

Round 11 As round 3.

Round 12 1ch, 1dc into same place as slip stitch, 1dc into each of next 7dc, 2dc into next dc, *1dc into each of next 8dc, 2dc into next dc, repeat from * to end; join with a slip stitch to first dc. 30dc.

Larger size only

Round 13 As round 3.

Round 14 1ch, 1dc into same place as slip stitch, 1dc into each of next 8dc, 2dc into next dc, *1dc into each of next 9dc, 2dc into next dc, repeat from * to end; join with a slip stitch to first dc. 33dc.

Both sizes

Work without shaping (as *round 3*) until slipper measures 11(14)cm/4^1/4(5^1/2)in – about 3(6) rounds.

Shape sole and sides

After joining with a slip stitch to first dc at end of last round as usual, work a slip stitch into each of the next 2dc. Turn the work.

Now work back and forth in rows for the rest of the slipper as follows:

Row 1 (wrong side) 1ch (this chain counts as first dc of row, so work it loosely), 1dc into each of next 15dc. Turn.

Row 2 1ch (to count as first dc), miss first dc and work 1dc into next dc, 1dc into each of remaining dc, work last dc into 1-ch at edge. Turn. 16dc.

Work 2(4) rows more as *row 2*.

Next row (increase row) 1ch (to count as first dc), 1dc into first dc, 1dc into each of remaining dc, 2dc into 1-ch at edge. Turn. 18dc.

Work 5 rows more as *row 2*, then repeat increase row once more. 20dc.

Continue in dc without increasing until work measures 24(27)cm/9^1/2(10^1/2)in or required foot length.

Fasten off (see Tips).

Work another slipper exactly the same.

TO FINISH

Pull the long loose end at the centre of each toe to tighten up the hole and weave it into at the inside of the slipper. Weave in any other loose ends inside the slipper as well.

Steam and press the slippers lightly.

Fold the heel end of the slipper in half, with wrong sides together, and join the back heel seam.

Edging

Using a 4.00mm hook and one strand of yarn and with the right side of the slipper facing, begin at back seam and work 1 row of dc along the slipper opening on each slipper. For an even edging, work 1dc into each row end along the sides of the opening, and 1dc into each dc along the front of the opening. Fasten off and weave in end.

Insoles

Cut a two pieces of felt to the same size as the insoles and glue one piece to the top of each insole using fabric glue. Leave to dry, then insert insoles into slippers.

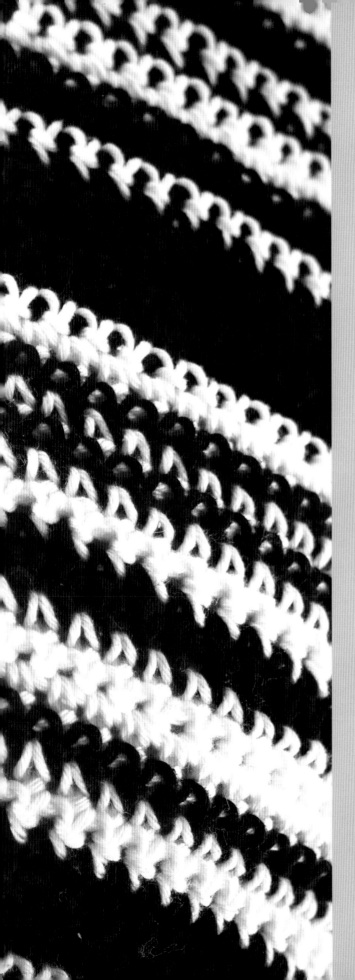

cafetière cover

No longer banished to the back of the kitchen drawer or cupboard, a tea cosy can take on a new guise – in this case as a sleek cover to keep the coffee warm at the breakfast table or in the office. This cafetière cover is worked in basic double crochet in a single colour, but would look equally good in a stripe. The shapings are worked just inside the edge to produce a smooth and rounded shape. The little knob can be made in a contrasting colour as an attractive finishing touch. To insulate the cover, line it with felt, which is widely available in most good craft stores.

COVER SIZE

Approximately 25cm/10in high x 21.5cm/8¾in wide (43cm/17½in in circumference). The cover is suitable for a small cafetière coffee pot.

MATERIALS

Plain cover

3 x 50g balls Rowan *Cotton Glacé* or a similar medium-weight mercerized cotton yarn (see page 126)

Hook size 3.00mm

Piece of of coloured felt for lining, 50cm x 30cm/20in x 12in

STITCH SIZE

This tea cosy has a 'tension' (stitch size) of 19 stitches and 23 rows to 10cm/4in measured over double crochet, but working to an exact tension is not essential (see Tips).

TECHNIQUES USED

Double crochet, simple decreases, joining in new balls of yarn and working in rounds.

TIPS

Tension

Don't worry about tension too much! Because this is a cafetière cosy, working to an exact size is not that important as long as the cosy will slip easily over your coffee pot.

Working in rounds

When you work your crochet in rounds you never have to turn the fabric. The right side is always facing you.

Marking the beginning of a round

Be sure to mark the beginning of each round to make it easier to keep your place.

Joining in a new yarn

This technique is used for changing yarns when your ball of yarn is finished or when you want to start a new colour for stripes. Change to a new yarn at the end of a row. Begin the last double crochet of the row in the usual way, by drawing a loop through the last stitch, then drop the old yarn and draw the new yarn through both loops now on the hook to finish the double crochet (see Crochet Basics). Leave a long loose end of the old and new yarns to weave in later, or work over the ends for several stitches before clipping them off.

METHOD

Front

Foundation chain Leaving a long loose end and using a 3.00mm hook, make 42 chain.

Row 1 Work 1dc into 3rd chain from hook, 1dc into each of remaining chain. Turn.

Row 2 1ch (this counts as first dc of row, so work it loosely), miss first dc and work 1dc into next dc, then work 1dc into each of remaining dc, work last dc into ch at edge. Turn. There are 41 stitches in the row.

Repeat *row 2* until work measures 17cm/6¾in from foundation-chain edge – a total of about 39 rows from beginning.

Top shaping

Begin shaping the top by decreasing one stitch at each end of the next row as follows:

Next row (decrease row) 1ch to count as first dc, miss first dc, 1dc into next dc, [insert hook into next dc, yarn round hook and draw a loop through] twice, yarn round hook and draw through all 3 loops on hook—called *decrease one stitch*—, work 1dc into each dc to last 4 stitches, then decrease one stitch by working next 2dc together as before, 1dc into each of last 2 stitches. Turn. 39dc.

Work one row without shaping (as *row 2*).
**Repeat the decrease row.
Work one row without shaping.** 37dc.
Repeat from ** to ** once more. 35dc.
Repeat the decrease row 12 times. 11dc.
Fasten off.

Back

Make another piece the same for the back of the cover.

TO FINISH

Weave in any loose ends at the back of the work. Lay the pieces out flat, then steam and press lightly.

Lining

Using one piece of the cosy as a template, cut out two pieces of felt to the same size and shape, but allowing an extra 1.5cm/⁵⁄₈in all around the curved edge for the seam allowance.

Place the crochet pieces together with the right sides facing each other, line up the stitches and pin. Then sew the pieces together and turn right side out.

Next, sew the lining pieces together and trim the seam. Place the lining inside the cosy, trim the bottom edge if necessary and stitch to the bottom edge of the cosy.

Bobble

For a detail that can be used to pull off the cover, make a little bobble as follows:

Foundation chain Leaving a long loose end and using a 3.00mm hook, make 2 chain.

Round 1 (right side) Work 6dc into 2nd chain from hook; join with a slip stitch to top of first dc of round.

Round 2 (right side) 1ch, place a short length of a contrasting yarn across your crochet fabric from front to back, tight up against the loop on the hook and above the working yarn—called *place marker*—, 2dc into same place as slip stitch was worked, 2dc into each of remaining 5dc of round; join with a slip stitch to first dc of round (ignore slip stitch and 1-ch and work into top of first dc – your marker marks the spot). There are now 12dc in the round.

Round 3 1ch, pull marker out of previous round and place marker as before, 1dc into same place as slip stitch, 1dc into each dc to end; join with a slip stitch to first dc. Continue to pull out your marker and place it at the beginning of each round.

Round 4 1ch, 1dc into same place as slip stitch, 2dc into the next dc, *1dc into next dc, 2dc into next dc, repeat from * to end; join with a slip stitch to first dc. 18dc.

Round 5 As round 3.

Round 6 1ch, 1dc into same place as slip stitch, *miss next dc, 1dc into next dc, repeat from * to last dc, miss last dc; join with a slip stitch to first dc. 9dc.
Stuff bobble with small amount of matching yarn to pad it.

Round 7 1ch, 1dc into same place as slip stitch, *miss next dc, 1dc into next dc, repeat from * to end. 5dc.
Fasten off leaving a long length of yarn. Use the long end to sew the opening closed, then stitch to the top of the cover.

towel edging

Crochet edgings add a touch of femininity to plain towels or bedlinen. This simple, easy-to-make edging can either be crocheted as a separate strip and slip-stitched onto a towel, or worked directly into the hem of the towel. Although the towel and edging here are both in natural, crisp white cotton, you can work the crochet edging in any colour and weight of yarn you like.

making : the towel edging

EDGING SIZE

The edging is approximately 3cm/1¼in deep and can be made to fit any size towel – the towel pictured is 66cm/26in wide (see Tips).

MATERIALS

1 x 25g ball of fine cotton yarn (enough for two strips of edging 66cm/26in long)
Hook size 1.75mm
Cotton towel of your choice (or alternative item to trim)

STITCH SIZE

This edging has a 'tension' (stitch size) of 24 stitches (6 scallops) to 10cm/4in measured over edging pattern, but working

to an exact tension is not essential (see Tips for more information).

TECHNIQUES USED

Double crochet, treble crochet, working into a chain loop and making picots.

TIPS

Tension and edging measurements
Don't worry about tension too much! The size of your edging will depend on the thickness of the yarn, and if your yarn is slightly thinner or thicker than the one used here, your tension may not match the one given above. Test your tension before starting the edging. Make 34 chain and work the edging pattern from *row 1*.

If your stitch size is different than the one recommended, then use your swatch to determine how many scallops you'll need to fit your towel.

Working into a chain loop
When working the last row of the scallop edging, work the double crochet into the chain loop by inserting hook *under* the chain – not *into* it. This covers the chain completely and gives the scallop a 'bound' look for an ornate edge.

Crocheting into the towel edge
If the weave of your towel is loose enough and your hook fine enough to pierce the towel, you can work your edging directly onto the towel. Work a multiple of 4 double crochet, plus 1 double crochet

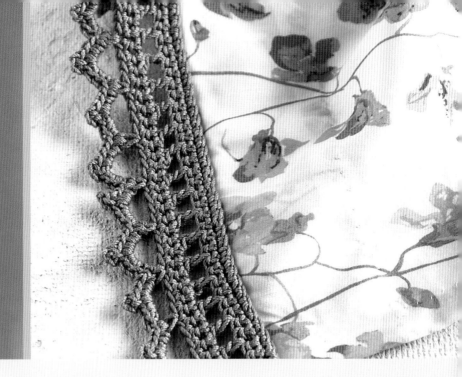

Try working your crochet lace edgings with linen or silk threads for a touch of luxury and contrast. Play with using coloured yarns as well. Then think of alternative projects to trim, such as pillowslips, cushions, sheets and duvets. Even curtains can be given a bohemian vintage look. For quick-to-make edgings, experiment with thicker yarns, and for delicate items, use finer threads.

extra, evenly along the edge – this will give one scallop for every 4dc worked. Then turn the work and start following the edging pattern from *row 2*.

METHOD

Foundation chain Determine how many scallops you need (see tips); then leaving a long loose end and using a 1.75mm hook, make a multiple of 4 chain (4 chain for each scallop) plus 2 extra. (For the 66cm/26in wide towel shown, 39 scallops were worked onto a foundation chain of 158 chain.)

Row 1 Work 1dc into 2nd chain from hook, 1dc into each of remaining chain. Turn.

Row 2 1ch, 1dc into each dc to end. Turn.

Row 3 Work 4ch to count as first tr and first 1-ch space, miss first 2dc, 1tr into next dc, *1ch, miss next dc, 1tr into next dc, repeat from * to end. Turn.

Row 4 1ch, 1dc into first tr, *1dc into next 1-ch space (inserting hook *under* the chain – not *into* the chain – when working the dc), 1dc into next tr, repeat from * to turning chain at end of row, 1dc into turning-chain space, 1dc into 2nd chain from last tr. Turn.

Row 5 1ch, 1dc into each dc to end. Turn.

Row 6 1ch, 1dc into first dc, *6ch, miss next 3dc, 1dc into next dc, repeat from * to end. Turn.

Row 7 (picot row) 1ch, 1dc into first dc, [3dc, 3ch (for picot), 3dc] all into each 6ch-loop to end (see Tips), 1dc into last dc. Fasten off.

This completes the edging.

Work another piece in the same way for the other end of the towel.

TO FINISH

Weave in any loose ends. Steam edging gently to flatten. Pin the edgings to the ends of the towel, slightly stretching or easing in if necessary, and oversew securely in place.

raffia table mats

Made in a simple crochet cluster pattern with richly coloured green raffia, these rectangular mats are ideal for informal meals or for eating al fresco. They are one of the easiest projects in this book to make – one mat should take you no longer than a few hours at most. As the pattern is so basic, you could make them on the bus or train.

making : the raffia table mats

TABLE MAT SIZE

Approximately 46cm x 35cm/18in x 13¾in (see Tips).

MATERIALS

Raffia for a set of four table mats (buy one ball from a craft store or stationers and test it to see how far it will go)
Hooks size 4.00mm and 5.00mm

STITCH SIZE

These mats have a 'tension' (stitch size) of approximately 8 clusters and 8 cluster rows to 10cm/4in measured over the cluster stitch pattern, but working to an exact tension is not essential (see Tips for more information)

TECHNIQUES USED

Simple treble-crochet clusters, double crochet edging and joining in new balls of raffia.

TIPS

Working the foundation chain

Be sure to use a larger hook for the foundation chain, so that the starting edge is not too tight. This will help the mat lay flat.

Tension

Achieving an exact tension is not essential, as you can easily alter the number of clusters and rows you work (see Inspiration box at the top of the opposite page for how to do this).

Joining in a new ball

This technique is used for joining in a new ball of raffia when your old one runs out or for changing colours when working stripes. Work your cluster in the usual way, but change to the new ball of yarn when drawing through the last loop that joins the 3-tr group at the top. Leave a long loose end of the old raffia and the new raffia to weave in later.

METHOD

Foundation chain Leaving a long loose end and using a 5.00mm hook, make 74 chain.

Change to a 4.00mm hook and begin the cluster stitch pattern as follows:

Row 1 [Wrap yarn round hook and insert hook through 4th chain from hook, yarn round hook and draw a loop through, yarn round hook and draw through first 2 loops on hook] twice (working each st into the same chain), yarn round hook and draw through all 3 loops on hook—this completes the *beginning cluster*—, *1ch, miss 1ch, [yarn round hook and insert hook into next ch, yarn round hook and draw a loop through, yarn round hook and draw through first 2 loops on hook] 3 times (working each st into the same chain), yarn round hook and draw through all 4 loops on hook—this completes the *cluster*—, repeat from * to end of

foundation chain. Turn. There are 36
clusters across the row.

Row 2 Work 3ch to count as first st in
beginning cluster, [wrap yarn round hook
and insert hook through top of first cluster
in previous row, yarn round hook and draw
a loop through, yarn round hook and draw
through first 2 loops on hook] twice
(working each st into the top of the same
cluster), yarn round hook and draw
through all 3 loops on hook—this
completes the *beginning cluster*—, *1ch,
[yarn round hook and insert hook through
top of next cluster, yarn round hook and
draw a loop through, yarn round hook and
draw through first 2 loops on hook] 3
times (working each st into the top of the
same cluster stitch), yarn round hook and
draw through all 4 loops on hook—this
completes the *cluster*—, repeat from * to
end of row. Turn.

Repeat *row 2* until the mat measures

about 34cm/13$^1/_4$in from the foundation-
chain edge (a total of about 27 rows from
beginning). Fasten off.

Make three more mats in the same way to
complete the set.

TO FINISH

Weave in any loose ends at the back of
each mat.

If it is necessary to flatten it, lay the table
mat out flat and leave overnight under a
pile of books.

Edging

Using a 4.00mm hook, work a row of
double crochet around the edge of each
mat. Both sides of the mats are the same –
which means there is no right side or
wrong side – so you can work the edging
with either side facing you.

For an even edging, work 1dc into each
chain along the foundation chain edge; 1dc
into each ch and 1dc into each cluster

along the top of the last row; 2dc into
each row end along the short sides;
and 3dc into each corner to keep the
mat square.

Fasten off and weave in end.

tea cosy

Retro-style crochet is back, re-invented. This little teapot cover is a timeless classic. Worked in double crochet in bright random stripes of colour in mercerized cotton, it is lined with contrasting gingham fabric and insulated with wadding. A little, curled, crocheted stem at the top adds a finishing touch, doubling up as useful handle.

COSY SIZE

Approximately 22cm/8³/₄in high x
31.5cm/12⁵/₈in wide (63cm/25¹/₄in in
circumference). The cosy is suitable for a
small teapot.

MATERIALS

Rowan *Cotton Glacé* or a similar
medium-weight mercerized cotton yarn
(see page 122) in 8 contrasting colours
as follows:

Colour A: 1 x 50g ball in purple
Colour B: 1 x 50g ball in black
Colour C: 1 x 50g ball in white
Colour D: 1 x 50g ball in turquoise
Colour E: 1 x 50g ball in light sage
Colour F: 1 x 50g ball in dark sage
Colour G: 1 x 50g ball in pink
Colour H: 1 x 50g ball in orange
Hook size 3.00mm
Piece of wadding to insulate cosy

30cm/12in of 112cm/44in wide black
and white gingham fabric for lining

STITCH SIZE

This tea cosy has a 'tension' (stitch size) of
19 stitches and 23 rows to 10cm/4in
measured over double crochet, but working
to an exact tension is not essential (see Tips).

TECHNIQUES USED

Double crochet, simple decreases and
joining in new balls of yarn.

TIPS

Tension
Don't worry about tension too much!
Because this is a tea cosy, working to an
exact size is not that important as long as
the cosy will slip easily over your teapot.

Joining in a new yarn
This technique is used for changing yarns

when your ball of yarn is finished or when
you want to start a new colour for stripes.
Change to a new yarn at the end of a row
on the tea cosy. Begin the last double
crochet of the row in the usual way, by
drawing a loop through the last dc, then
drop the old yarn and draw the new yarn
through both loops now on the hook to
finish the double crochet (see Crochet
Basics). Leave a long loose end of the old
and new yarns to weave in later, or work
over the ends for several stitches before
clipping them off.

INSPIRATION

Experiment with different yarn textures
and/or different colour combinations for
your tea cosy. For a homemade touch,
work your tea cosy in random black and
white cotton stripes and line with bold
black and white ticking.

METHOD

Front

Foundation chain Leaving a long loose end and using a 3.00mm hook and colour A (purple), make 61 chain.

Row 1 Using A (purple), work 1dc into 2nd chain from hook, 1dc into each of remaining chain, dropping A and drawing through B (black) when completing last loop of last dc of row (see Tips). Turn. There are 60 stitches in the row.

Row 2 Using B (black), 1ch, 1dc into each dc to end of row. Turn.

Continuing to repeat *row 2* to form the double crochet fabric and changing colours with the last loop of the row before, work in stripes as follows:

Colour B (black): 1 row.
Colour C (white): 1 row.
Colour B (black): 1 row.
Colour D (turquoise): 3 rows.
Colour E (light sage): 1 row.
Colour F (dark sage): 2 rows.
Colour G (pink): 5 rows.
Colour H (orange): 2 rows.
Colour B (black): 2 rows.
Colour E (light sage): 1 row.
Colour B (black): 1 row.
Colour E (light sage): 2 rows.
Colour D (turquoise): 1 row.

Top shaping

Using D (turquoise), begin shaping the top by decreasing one stitch at each end of the next row as follows:

Next row (decrease row) Insert hook into first dc, yarn round hook and draw a loop through, insert hook into next dc, yarn round hook and draw a loop through, yarn round hook and draw through all 3 loops on hook—called *decrease one stitch*—, work 1dc each dc to last 2dc,

then decrease one stitch by working last 2dc together as before. Turn. 58dc.

Repeating the decrease row when instructed, continue working double crochet in stripes as follows:

Using colour C (white), work one row in without shaping (as *row 2*).

[Using colour F (dark sage), repeat decrease row, then work one row without shaping] twice. 54dc.

Still using colour F (dark sage), repeat decrease row. 52dc.

Using colour E (light sage), work one row in without shaping, then repeat decrease row. 50dc.

Using colour A (purple), repeat decrease row. 48dc.

Using colour C (white), repeat decrease row. 46dc.

Using colour H (orange), work one row without shaping.

Using colour B (black), repeat decrease row, then work one row without shaping. 44dc.

Using colour A (purple), repeat decrease row twice. 40dc.

Using colour G (pink), repeat decrease row twice, then work one row without shaping. 36dc.

Using colour C (white), repeat decrease row. 34dc.

Using colour B (black), repeat decrease row twice. 30dc.

Using colour E (light sage), repeat decrease row twice, then work one row without shaping. 26dc.

Still using colour E (light sage), slip stitch to last 2dc.

Fasten off.

Back

Make another piece the same for the back of the tea cosy.

TO FINISH

Weave in any loose ends at the back of the work.

Lay the pieces out flat, then steam and press lightly.

Lining

Using one piece of the cosy as a template, cut out two pieces of lining fabric to the same size and shape, but allowing an extra 1.5cm/⅝in all around each piece for the seam allowance. Cut two pieces of wadding the same shape and size as the lining pieces.

Place the crochet pieces together with the right sides facing each other, line up the stitches and pin. Then sew the pieces together and turn right side out.

Place the fabric lining pieces together with the right sides facing each other and sew together along the curved edge. Sew the wadding pieces together in the same way and trim the seams.

Place the wadding inside the crocheted tea cosy and trim the bottom edge to the same length as the tea cosy. Then place the lining inside. Turn up the hem of the lining all around the bottom edge and join to the cosy edge with small, neat stitches.

Stem

For a functional detail that can be used to pull off the tea cosy, make a little stalk as follows:

Using the colour of your choice and a 3.00mm hook, make 10 chain.

Work 6 rows of double crochet and fasten off.

Allowing the crochet to roll in on itself, sew the foundation-chain edge to the last row to form a curled tube shape.

Stitch the stem securely to the top of the cosy.

runner

For informal meals with friends, eating al fresco, or for relaxed
parties, set out a runner on the floor, or on a long low table, with
platters of food. This simple runner is worked in string in double
crochet with borders of coloured linen yarn – a modern variation
on a traditional piece. If you prefer, work the borders in bright
contrasting colours.

The stylish strip border on the runner forms interesting details at the corners. But if you're in a hurry, you can add a simpler border by working double crochet round and round the string rectangle, mitring the corners as you go. For an even edging, work 1dc into each stitch or row end and 3dc at each corner for the mitre. Add stripes, or work just the final row in a contrasting colour for a smart finishing detail.

making : the runner

RUNNER SIZE
Approximately 40cm x 146cm/16in x 58½in.

MATERIALS
7 x 85m/93yd balls thick parcel string (available from local hardware stores or stationers)
Rowan *Cotton Glacé* or a similar lightweight cotton or linen yarn (see page 122) in 4 contrasting colours as follows:
Colour A: 2 x 50g balls in yellow
Colour B: 2 X 50g balls in charcoal
Colour C: 1 X 50g balls in olive
Colour D: 1 x 50g balls in pale olive
Hook sizes 5.00mm and 6.00mm

STITCH SIZE
This runner has a 'tension' (stitch size) of 11 stitches and 14 rows to 10cm/4in

measured over double crochet and using a single strand of string or two strands of lightweight yarn – but working to an exact tension is not essential (see Tips).

TECHNIQUES USED
Double crochet, simple borders and joining in new balls of yarn.

TIPS
Working the foundation chain
Be sure to use a larger hook for the foundation row, so that the starting edge is not too tight. This will help the runner to lay flat.

Tension and runner size
Don't worry about tension too much! Because this is a runner, an exact size is not that important as long as it suits your table. You can make the runner to

any length you want by adding to or subtracting from the number of foundation chain, and to any width by working more or fewer rows.

Using yarn double
The coloured linen yarns are used double throughout. If the colour only calls for one ball of yarn, wind the ball off into two balls so it is ready to use double.

Joining in a new yarn
This technique is used for starting a new ball of yarn. Begin a double crochet in the usual way, by drawing a loop through the next stitch, then drop the old yarn and draw the new yarn through both loops now on the hook to finish the double crochet. Leave a long loose end of the old and new yarns to weave in later, or work over the ends for several stitches before clipping them off.

Joining on new colours for borders
When joining on a new colour for the borders, insert the hook through the first stitch and draw a loop through, then continue as usual in double crochet, repeating *row 2* of the pattern.

METHOD

Foundation chain Leaving a long loose end and using a 6.00mm hook and string, make 154 chain.
Change to a 5.00mm hook and begin working in double crochet as follows:
Row 1 Work 1dc into 2nd chain from hook, 1dc into each of remaining chain. Turn.
Row 2 1ch (this counts as first dc of row, so work it loosely), miss first dc and work 1dc into next dc, then work 1dc into each of remaining dc, work last dc into 1-ch

at edge. Turn. There are 154 stitches in the row.
Repeat *row 2* until work measures 34cm/13^1/$_2$in from foundation-chain edge – a total of about 46 rows from beginning. Fasten off.

Borders
Using a 5.00mm hook and colour A (yellow) double, join yarn to last row worked and work 6 rows in double crochet along this edge. (See Tips for joining on new colours for borders.)
Fasten off.
Using a 5.00mm hook and colour B (charcoal) double, join yarn to foundation-chain edge and work 6 rows in double crochet along this edge. Fasten off.
Using a 5.00mm hook and colour C (olive) double, join yarn to one short end and work 6 rows in double crochet along this

edge. (For an even border, work 1dc into each row end.) Fasten off.
Work 6 rows in double crochet along the other short end in the same way, but using colour D (pale olive).

TO FINISH
Weave any loose ends into the double crochet.
Lay the work out flat, then steam and press lightly.

useful information

The section on Crochet Basics on pages 14–27 shows you how to work the most basic stitches in crochet. The following information may be helpful to you when creating crochet projects, either from this book or any other patterns you find.

You can choose to use the recommended yarns given at the beginning of the instructions to each project, or you can substitute others (see page 122 for information on yarn weights and types so you can choose suitable alternatives). Whether you choose to use the recommended yarns, or ones of your own choice, you must check that you are working to the appropriate tension, or the item you are making may turn out a very different size! See pages 16 and 17 for information on checking tension.

Having said that, if you are making a throw, for example, and do not mind too much if it is a little bigger or smaller than the one shown in the pattern, then do not overly worry about the tension. This is true of cushions, too, unless you wish to create a cover to fit a specific-sized cushion pad, when, of course, the tension and the finished size will be important.

Certain yarns are easier to crochet with than others; those that are pliable and soft on the hands are the best for beginners, so select projects with soft cotton yarns to start with. Crocheting with string is not difficult, but as it is less pliable and elastic than cotton it takes a little more dexterity initially, as indeed does leather, which benefits from being warmed before use.

PATTERN INFORMATION

The instructions for crochet projects are usually given in writing. The basic abbreviations used in pattern writing are shown opposite, although these can vary, so always check the abbreviations guide in any crochet book first. One area of potential confusion is that US terminology is different from UK terminology. In the US, double crochet is called single crochet, for example, while treble crochet is known as double crochet and so on.

In some instances in crochet it is easier to present the pattern information in charted form. This is particularly true of filet crochet where the pattern forms a grid, and can be most easily understood from a chart drawn on graph paper. Each 'block' or 'space' is represented by one square of the graph.

Most patterns have elements that repeat. There is an asterisk at the beginning of the repeat element of the pattern, or it is placed inside two asterisks or brackets. The number of times this sequence is repeated is indicated outside the asterisks or brackets, along with any additional stitches required to complete a row.

PRACTICE MAKES PERFECT

You will find that the speed and ease with which you crochet is simply a matter of practice. It is a good idea to test your skills on very simple stitches, possibly making a few tension squares first. (You can always stitch them together later to make a patchwork cushion!)

ABBREVIATIONS

To make the instructions for the crochet patterns easier to follow for beginners, very few abbreviations have been used. However, the following lists cover the main abbreviations you may come across in other patterns as well:

abbreviations for crochet stitches

ch	chain
dc	double crochet
dtr	double treble
htr	half treble
qtr	quadruple treble
sl st	slip stitch
tr	treble
trtr	triple treble

other abbreviations

alt	alternate
approx	approximately
beg	begin(ning)
cm	centimetre(s)
cont	continu(e)(ing)
dec	decreas(e)(ing)
foll	follow(s)(ing)
g	gramme(s)
in	inch(es)
inc	increas(e)(ing)
m	metre(s)
mm	millimetre(s)
oz	ounce(s)
patt(s)	pattern(s)
rem	remain(s)(ing)
rep	repeat(s)(ing)
RS	right side
st(s)	stitch(es)
tog	together
WS	wrong side
yd	yard(s)
yrh	yarn round hook
*	Repeat instructions after asterisk or between asterisks as many times as instructed.
[]	Repeat instructions inside brackets as many times as instructed.

CROCHET HOOKS

Here is a conversion chart for the various systems of hook sizes – just in case you have old hooks you'd like to use but aren't sure what they are equivalent to.

hook conversion chart

Metric	US	old UK
.60mm	14 steel	
.75mm	12 steel	
1.00mm	11 steel	
1.50mm	8 steel	
1.75mm	6 steel	
2.00mm	B/1	14
2.50mm	C/2	12
3.00mm	D/3	10
3.50mm	E/4	9
4.00mm	F/5	8
4.50mm	G/6	7
5.00mm	H/8	6
5.50mm	I/9	5
6.00mm	J/10	4
6.50mm		3
7.00mm	K/10	2
8.00mm	L/11	
9.00mm	N/13	
10.00mm	P/15	
16.00mm	Q	

substituting yarns

Although I have recommended a specific yarn for many of the projects in the book, you can substitute others. A description of each of the yarns used is given below.

If you decide to use an alternative yarn, any other make of yarn that is of the same weight and type should serve as well, but to avoid disappointing results, it is very important that you test the yarn first.

Purchase a substitute yarn that is as close as possible to the original in thickness, weight and texture so that it will be compatible with the crochet instructions. Buy only one ball to start with, so you can try out the effect. Calculate the number of balls you will need by meterage/yardage rather than by weight. The recommended knitting-needle size and knitting tension/gauge on the ball bands are extra guides to the yarn thickness.

Alongside the manufacturer's brand name and the name given to the specific yarn, a ball band will typically carry the following information:

Recommended tension/gauge and needle/hook sizes
This is the recommended tension/gauge and needle or hook size, however a designer may vary from this recommendation within a pattern. If so, always go with the designer's recommendation.

Weight of yarn
Given in grams in the UK and ounces in the US, most yarns come in either 50g or 100g balls.

Meterage
This is the approximate length of yarn in the ball and is just as important to consider as tension when considering a substitute yarn.

Fibre composition
A ball band will list the materials that the yarn is made from, whether that is 100% pure wool or a blend of fibres such as cotton and silk. This affects not just the method of care for the finished item, but also the suitability of a yarn for a certain project.

Shade and dye-lot numbers
Each shade of yarn is given an identifying name and/or number by the manufacturer. When purchasing yarn the dye-lot number is equally, if not more, important as this number needs to be the same on every ball. As yarn is dyed in batches, buying yarn with the same dye-lot numbers ensures there will be no colour variations between balls.

Care instructions
A ball band will indicate whether the yarn is suitable for machine washing or is dry clean only, and whether or not it can be ironed and, if so, at what temperature. This information is usually given in the form of internationally recognised standard care symbols.

WOOL AND COTTON YARNS

Rowan All Seasons Cotton

A medium-weight (aran-weight) cotton yarn with a soft, lofty texture

Recommended knitting-needle size: $4^{1}/_{2}$–$5^{1}/_{2}$mm/US 7–9

Tension/gauge: 16–18 sts x 23–25 rows per 10cm/4in over knitted stocking stitch

Ball size: 90m/98yd per 50g/$1^{3}/_{4}$oz ball

Yarn specification: cotton blend; 16 shades

Rowan Cotton Glacé

A medium-weight (between double knitting and 4 ply) mercerized cotton yarn

Recommended knitting-needle size: $3^{1}/_{4}$–$3^{3}/_{4}$mm/US 3–5

Tension/gauge: 23 sts x 32 rows per 10cm/4in over knitted stocking stitch

Ball size: 115m/126yd per 50g/$1^{3}/_{4}$oz ball

Yarn specification: 100% cotton; 24 shades

Rowan Handknit Cotton

A medium-weight (double-knitting-weight) yarn

Recommended knitting-needle size: 4–$4^{1}/_{2}$mm/US 6–7

Tension/gauge: 19–20 sts x 28 rows per 10cm/4in over knitted stocking stitch

Ball size: 85m/93yd per 50g/$1^{3}/_{4}$oz ball

Yarn specification: 100% cotton; 26 shades

Rowan Siena 4ply

A lightweight (4-ply) cotton yarn

Recommended knitting-needle size: $2^{3}/_{4}$–3mm/US 2–3

Tension/gauge: 28 sts x 38 rows per 10cm/4in over knitted stocking stitch

Ball size: 140m/153yd per 50g/$1^{3}/_{4}$oz ball

Yarn specification: 100% cotton; 20 shades

Twilleys Goldfingering

A fine metallic-effect yarn

Recommended knitting-needle size: $2^{3}/_{4}$–$3^{1}/_{4}$mm/US 3

Tension/gauge: 29–34 sts x 36–40 rows per 10cm/4in over knitted stocking stitch

Ball size: 175m/191yd per 25g/1oz ball

Yarn specification: viscose blend; 4 shades

OTHER YARNS

Fine cotton threads specially designed for crochet lace are widely available in craft shops. The cotton thread used for the lace edging on pages 102–105 was obtained from:

Yeoman Yarns Ltd

Tel: 0116 2404464

www.yeoman-yarns.co.uk

Leather thonging is available in craft stores or from leather merchants/saddlery shops. The 2mm-thick round leather thonging used for the basket on pages 84–87 and the floor cushion on pages 38–41 was obtained from:

J.T. Batchelor Ltd

Tel: 020 7254 2962

www.jtbatchelor.co.uk

String comes in various thicknesses and is not always labelled with an exact amount, so you may need to experiment with a single ball to start with. The round cushion (pages 30–33), the boxes (pages 76–79), the bottle cover (pages 80–83) and the runner (pages 114–117) are made with parcel string, which comes either in 40m/44yd or 85m/93m balls, available from Muji and stationers.

The coloured polypropylene string used for the string bag on pages 88–91 comes in 89m/yd balls and is available from B&Q and stationers.

care of crochet

If you have taken the time and trouble to create your own crochet textiles, you will want to make sure that they remain in good condition. The great variety of yarns on the market has necessitated some kind of international labelling standards for their care, which is normally indicated on the ball band of the yarn. While some yarns can be successfully dry cleaned (check the symbols on the ball bands), many more are better washed carefully by hand. A few can be machine washed at appropriate temperatures. Again, all this information should be on the ball band.

HAND WASHING GUIDELINES

• If the article requires hand washing, then make sure that you use soap flakes which must be dissolved before emersing it. Do not use very hot water to wash any woollen yarn. Hand hot temperatures are best.

• Always rinse the article at least twice in tepid water.

• Don't wring it roughly by hand; it is best to give it a short spin in the machine or, with delicate yarns, to wrap it in a towel and squeeze out the moisture gently.

• Pull the article gently into shape and hang it over a towel to dry, preferable on a flat surface.

MACHINE WASHING GUIDELINES

The temperature guidelines found on machines are as follows:

60°C/140°F hot: Hotter than the hand can bear; the temperature of most domestic hot water
50°C/120°F hand hot: As hot as the hand can stand
40°C/104°F warm: Just warm to the touch
30°C/86°F cool: Cool to the touch

CARE OF SPECIAL YARNS

• Mercerized cotton, soft cotton and fine cotton are best washed by hand. Rinse well. Squeeze gently in a towel to remove surplus moisture and hang flat to dry.

• Heavier weight cottons can be washed in a machine on a cool wash; check the ball band label. Short spin only. Dry flat.

• Lurex, mohair and chenille are best dry cleaned in certain solvents. Check with your dry cleaner. Air well after cleaning.

• String, leather, sisal, hemp and raffia cannot normally be dry cleaned and are best sponged down with a damp cloth and left to dry naturally.

index

other books by Erika Knight

SIMPLE KNITTING
A how-to-knit workshop with 20 desirable projects
photography by Yuki Sugiura

Simple Knitting is a how-to-knit book that will teach you the core stitches and techniques while you create an enviable collection of hand-knitted items. Through a series of work-shop-style masterclasses Erika Knight explains the essential know-how – from achieving a perfect tension and substituting yarns to shaping and finishing a garment perfectly – alongside broader design principles, such as selecting yarns and building a colour palette. *Simple Knitting* is the ultimate learn-to-knit book.

CROCHET WORKSHOP
Learn how to crochet with 20 inspiring projects
photography by Yuki Sugiura

Get hooked on crochet with Erika Knight's *Crochet Workshop*. Each of the 20 projects in this book teaches you a new skill and builds on techniques already learned in the preceding projects. Erika begins with simple crochet, before taking you through double and treble crochet and then moves on to the more intricate stitches. Under Erika Knight's guidance you will soon be making gorgeous projects.

NATURAL NURSERY KNITS
20 hand-knit projects for the new baby
photography by Kristin Perers

Ranging from first garments through to blankets, cushions and toys, with *Natural Nursery Knits* Erika Knight has created a charming collection of 20 irresistible designs. They provide all the hand knits a newborn needs in his or her first months: a classic cardigan, cosy first blanket, practical Initialled washcloth, whimsical bird mobile, and even a quintessential teddy bear, are all included. Create beautiful and practical items that will cosset your baby in those first months or make something to give as a gift that is sure to be cherished for years to come.

ESSENTIAL CROCHET
30 irresistible projects for you and your home
photography by Graham Atkins Hughes

Divided into five chapters – Basic, Timeless, Contemporary, Heirloom and Vintage – the 30 projects in this fabulous book embrace both new and traditional techniques within crochet, from a delicate filet pillow to a striking leather tote bag or round rose cushion. An introductory section leads the beginner through the basics, or provides a welcome refresher for those enticed back to this craft.

MEN'S KNITS: A NEW DIRECTION
A collection of 20 hand knits for men
photography by Chris Terry

Erika Knight presents a capsule collection of 20 hand knits for men that are practical and comfortable as well as distinctive and stylish. The collection is divided into four sections – Basics, Items, New Classics and Accessories – but all are based around a highly wearable neutral palette complemented by accent colours. The instructions for each garment are given in a range of sizes – from small to XXL – and schematics detail the key measurements. Photographed on men aged between 17 and 71, several of the projects are shown in alternative colourways and all are worn with inimitable style.

KEEP CALM & CAST ON
Good advice for knitters

Keep Calm & Cast On is the essential, inexpensive pocket-sized gift for any knitter. Packed full of tips and quotes, this book is guaranteed to keep the contemporary knitter calm in the face of any dropped stitch. Alongside the witticisms and facts is solid, practical advice designed to keep the knitter sane. It may be small, but this book ensures that you will never again get your knitting in a big tangle.

For further information of all of Erika Knight's books and yarn collection, go to www.erikaknight.co.uk.

Quadrille *craft*

Creative craft books for modern makers

www.quadrillecraft.co.uk

If you have any comments or queries regarding the instructions in this book, please contact us at enquiries@quadrille.co.uk

acknowledgements

I would like to thank Susan Berry for sharing the vision, John Heseltine for his discerning eye, Anne Wilson for her elegant design, Sally Harding for her professionalism, Sally Lee for her perfectionism, enthusiasm and tireless hard work (well, everything), Hannah Davis for her wisdom and generosity of spirit, and Julia Bird for her inherent style. I would also like to thank Quadrille for 'seeing it': in particular Jane O'Shea, for her unfailing encouragement and support, and Mary Evans and Helen Lewis for offering a guiding hand. I am grateful, too, to Stephen Sheard of Coats plc (Rowan and Jaeger yarns) for his enthusiastic and continued support, and to Ann Hinchcliffe for her patience and efficiency. Above all, I would like to thank my loving, long-suffering family and friends for their support, and the suppers! You all made it happen, thank you!